SALVAGE

#13
GIVE DUST A TONGUE

AUTUMN / WINTER 2022

And finally, Capital by Karl Marx,
which I read at the age of 18.

Contents

Two contributions from *Salvage*'s panel, 'Freedom in the Twenty-first Century', at the 2022 Historical Materialism conference in London:

RICHARD SEYMOUR

Literally Nothing: Sick in the Heart of Working-Class Life

I. Start with the unspeakable. There is, as Simon Charlesworth puts it in his phenomenology of working-class experience, a 'vulnerability-bound inarticulateness' in class life. Andrew Sayer, writing on the moral significance of class, describes a mute, 'low-level shame', just below the threshold of articulacy. Diane Reay, in her study of working-class schoolgirls, finds a dread of amounting – in the words of one student – to 'literally nothing'. Working-class women, Beverley Skeggs finds, often reject the identification with class, fearing that it labels them as vulgar, and socially unacceptable. In their studies of class identification, Michael Savage and his colleagues at the London School of Economics found persistent patterns of evasion, of an unwillingness to identify with a class – most strongly among those who are most disempowered. But the middle class, too, is wary, liable to qualify class identifications with stories of personal overcoming, effort, and upward mobility.

It is not that people are unaware of the gigantic inequalities that determine life, but that the language of class often doesn't hit home, viscerally, as an explanation. Adam Ashforth, in his study of witchcraft in post-apartheid South Africa, describes a 'structure of plausibility' within which the sleights and difficulties of life might be experienced as a 'spiritual injustice' inflicted by envious, wicked others in the community. And what it means when class is a less structurally plausible explanation than spiritual predation, when patient class hate is less resonant than the reactive emotions borne of helplessness – *the cosmopolitan elites, the immigrants, the bossy do-gooders, the selfish unions, the Muslims, the trans women, they're the ones that are doing this to me* – is that the institutions of class consciousness have withered to a few fine, pale stems.

In his essay, 'Old Gods, New Enigmas: Notes on Revolutionary Agency', Mike Davis describes the complex processes of class formation in the fin-de-siècle socialist movement: the mass literature, from *L'Humanité, Avanti!, New York Call, Wahre Jakob*, and *El Socialista* to *Pravda*. The Workers' Palaces, Mechanics Institutes, reading rooms, libraries and public lecture halls. The sports clubs, the institutions of self-help, the effortful civilising process aimed at producing workers who were capable of self-government, thus of freedom. As unattractively puritanical as all this frequently was, as unrealistic was its tendency to calibrate personal conduct in relation to the historical criteria of the class struggle, it sought to create workers who were fit, confident, knowledgeable, dignified, capable of long, fruitful lives, and equal to the intimidation, violence and setbacks of prolonged struggle to achieve self-rule. And, being founded on a 'scientific' socialism, a Marxist method that analysed the power of capitalist imperatives – the power of violent abstractions to run people's lives – it undercut personalised resentment, the allure of witchcraft.

☭

II. What we are left with, in the absence of this, is class shame. But it cannot be acknowledged as such, because we're ashamed of being ashamed. One form of repression is to detach thought from the affect it produces. So, you have the thought, but dismiss it. And the feeling, the mute sense of shame, lingers. You mitigate your existence around class superiors with exaggerated, apologetic niceness. You come over uneasy, with a prickly hot sweat, in a 'fancy' shop. You assume it's a personal inadequacy because it's felt as a personal inadequacy. You try to move on, be optimistic, find hope. But, says Charlesworth, the future is inaccessible to those under forty. He was writing in 2000, over two decades ago. 'The world they inhabit', he finds, 'is fractured, no longer supported by a steady stream of habitual associations, and their personal, affective world is pre-constituted as chaotic: absurd.' Hope is found, not in the fabric of an ever-more-precarious life-building, but in commodity form. From self-help to palingenetic nationalism.

Class life is work, and work doesn't start or stop at the workplace. Work is the locus of life-building – what we call our dreams – and of the shattering existential experiences of class.

☭

Allow me to represent, to you, myself at the age of twenty five. I had graduated, at that stage, from zero hours call-centre work to a regular, nine-to-five-thirty job, in a market research office. The work itself, though relentlessly tedious, wasn't the exhausting thing. Far worse were prolonged periods of having nothing to do, and having to invent tasks to avoid being assigned something even more demeaning and hateful. Then worse still, the office politics. The colleagues you can't stand or who you like but can't stand you. The junior managers who become a pain in the arse because you haven't flattered them, or have tried too hard, or in some way gave the impression of being a smartarse, or uppity, or of thinking you're too good for the job. The email exchanges with other departments, who want to blame you for their problems, or get you to do their work, or offload their misery, in the spirit of existential revenge. The productivity meetings with department heads or managers where, if you're as sophisticated and worldly as I was – slightly less so than Babbitt of Zenith, USA – you're amazed to find that it's the bosses who seemed most down to earth and human who single you out for particular humiliation over the most trivial of complaints. Those same managers, to your further astonishment, flirt with you in after-work socials.

The desolating rituals of 'fun': cake Tuesday, pub Wednesday, dress-down Friday, because Friday is funday – capitalism, having monopolised the best of the day, the glorious daylight hours, insists that you have fun. The dead zone of zombie labour, a separate time-stream, a slow, agonising current that registers change only by the occasional awareness that it's getting darker outside, and the best of the day is slipping away. The bleeding of the dead zone into free time. 'Flexibility', as though your willingness to do extra work is a fun fact about your personality. The commute in crowded trains and buses, the time it takes to unwind, to let go of whatever it was that had you crying in the toilet. The strange guilt you feel when you're ill and take a day off. And no one to stick up for you. Strikes are about as fashionable as shoulder pads. When you naively ask if there's a union they stiffly reply: 'we have no interest in a union'. They could hardly be more provoked if you gave them a stiff finger up the Celtic end.

The worst is the dawning interminability of it: it will *never* stop. It will only pause for holidays. It's what you have been des-tined for by an accident of birth, a chance swerve of the atom. And there's nothing to build with. The money is better than minimum wage, but not enough to rent more than a single room in a London house. Where is all this going anyway: what was the dream? And though you wore a suit the first week at work, you're now con-stantly late, resisting passively. A depression you barely perceive, let alone understand, is consoled with McDonald's breakfast food in the morning and booze at night. You're growing blotchy-skinned, pudgy and unfit, and you reek of unhappiness.

Every now and then, something reminds you of how little the world thinks of you, or how little you secretly think of yourself. Your bank abruptly cancels your overdraft, just a day before your money was coming in. They claim they've tried to contact you. They take it all. Your student loans company takes a payment. They claim they sent you the deferment forms. They take a third of your disposable income for the month. Or a bill comes that you weren't expecting. And it's worse because you should have known. It's all your own stupid fault. Now you have nothing to play with, nothing to have fun with, for the rest of the month. And when you try to negotiate with the bank, or the student loans company, they scold you. Their instant class evaluations, which are moral evaluations, permit them to humiliate you. Or, what if you're wrong? The problem with injustice is that you develop a highly sensitised apparatus for picking up on sleights, an unconscious apparatus that registers in others your own obscure feelings about yourself and your body.

And you should manage your money better. But money can be fleeting. Save, they say. For what? If you saved your whole life, you might get a mortgage for a dump in Plumstead, no offence. Defer gratification, they say. But you've been doing that the whole month until pay day; your whole life is an exercise in perpetually deferred gratification. There's nothing coming, except more work, more debt, and more of those fight-or-flight shocks. There is no future. You may as well enjoy it now.

Besides. You're a young working-class man. You have no idea how to take care of yourself. You wear shit, cheap shit that falls apart in a couple of months and needs to be replaced with more cheap shit. You don't understand fashion and its obscure sexual charisma, and you resent those who do, and anyway it's too expensive. You eat shit, because you don't know how to cook. You live in shit, because tidying a small rented room hardly seems worth the effort.

You eat shit, you wear shit, you live in shit, you're drinking your body to shit, you're treated like shit: you are shit.

☭

Failure in the neoliberal culture, whose axioms of competition in conditions of optimal stupidity are 'they're all out to get me' and 'nothing makes sense', is toxic. And, in conditions in which the means of life are increasingly black-boxed to increase dependency and suggestibility, we are increasingly deprived of even a fine margin of control over whether we succeed or fail. Hence the pervasive fear of 'adulting' among Millennials and Generation Z, laughed at in the newspapers as evidence of snowflake fragility, but actually evidence of disempowerment and the resulting dysphoria and apathy. Hence 'blackpilling', that whirlpool of reactive emotions that culminates in a desire for suicide-revenge on the world.

☭

III. This is one story of one point in one working life, characterised by absurdity, cluelessness, disorientation, in which the only predictability is more work. I mean to show something like the density of experience in which, as I say, work doesn't start or stop at the workplace.

Not simply because of our free after-hours labour, but because of the work, in the Freudian sense, that it has us doing. The work on our instinctual excitations, to use an antiquated idiom, which must be suitably sublimated and organised around the working day and keeping things going interminably. The belabouring of the self which often appears as a decoy, as compassionate guidance, tough love, self-help. When Freud wrote on *Civilization and Its Discontents* – that is, on the burdens that civilization imposed on drive-satisfactions – he didn't really have much to say about work. But it is probably the single major source of mental distress in the world today.

And when we talk of 'workplace stress', we are talking in part of psychosocial stress.

One of the Barthesian mythologies of workplace stress is that it particularly afflicts busy executives. The imagery: man in expensive suit, at an office desk, in front of a PC, pinching his nose, lowering his face into his hands, wiping his brow; doing anything with his hands but working; so unproductive. The Whitehall Studies showed us the exact opposite. The lower in the chain of authority you are, the less assertive you are, the less you take control of conversations, the less clearly you articulate, the higher your rate of stress, cardiovascular disease and mortality. The fight-or-flight responses triggered by petty injustices are cumulatively deadly, weakening your immune system, enlarging your adrenal gland, cutting your life expectancy.

Then there is the damage done by self-medicating for those class injuries, barely understood as such, often perceived more as a fatal form of moral non-recognition, which result in the famous 'deaths of despair'. You are not just stressed, anxious, suffocating, drowning, losing your hair, losing or gaining weight, suffering with heartburn, unable to orient yourself, unaware of where to put your feet: you are an orphan of history. And that's why mental illness is being politicised far more efficaciously by the Right, even as it's depoliticised by McMindfulness, CBT and other assorted panaceas.

The resentment bred by class experience can be dangerous. It can be a demoralising, self-destructive emotion. It has been said that resentment is like swallowing poison and waiting for the other chap to die. As Max Scheler wrote in *Ressentiment*, this sort of resentment doesn't seek restitution precisely because it is enthralled by its powerlessness, and the 'growing pleasure afforded by invective and negation'. It can also lead to explosions of violence, what Lacanians would call a 'passage to the act'. The 'lone wolf' contagion began, you might recall, with a spate of workplace shootings: it was called 'going postal'. The most miserably oppressed members of the workforce got a gun and went on the rampage, often singling out managers responsible for their petty humiliations. They received, from surviving co-workers, a surprising amount of sympathy.

It can also be profoundly reactionary.

Think of the 'shopkeepers' talk' described by Karen Wells and Sophie Watson, the idle pleasure taken in berating asylum seekers, minorities and big corporations, the consolation of moaning without solution. Think of the resentment for 'metropolitan elites' and the middle classes in far off London. Thomas Gorman's fieldwork on class resentment mainly finds working-class resentment directed at members of the middle class, by whom they feel patronised or belittled, or at an unfair disadvantage. Because while the mechanisms of class injury are abstract, and the ruling class remote from daily life, the middle class is experienced as a supervisory professional or managerial layer wielding authority.

This tendency to experience working class resentment through the more proximal, felt relationship with middle-class professionals might help explain why the rich can be so resented, as a recent analysis of class attitudes by Spencer Piston of Boston University suggests they are, yet reactionaries find it laughably easy to instead stimulate resentment against liberal professionals and left-wing students aspiring to be liberal professionals as if they were 'the metropolitan elite'.

Yet, we can't bypass these emotions, since they are engendered by the existential structures of life, by powers rendered obscure and unaccountable by their remoteness and abstraction, by worlds rendered incomprehensible to the point of absurdity. The strategic question is how to selectively provoke resentment, bring it to consciousness, or rather bring shame to consciousness and transform it into resentment, and educate it in the direction of a more sober, slow-burning, impersonal class hate; one that is patient, rigorous, humane, pluralist, anti-Manichaean and constructive. I think, on a modest scale, of how Bernie Sanders campaigns in the United States, linking resentment toward billionaires and the rich with demands like a fifteen dollar minimum wage, and contrast it ruefully with the priestly pieties of 'the politics of kindness' and 'they go low, we go high'.

Not that kindness and the high road are undesirable, not that this hasn't been a desideratum of the socialist movement since its inception, and not that we could or should imitate the Right's relentless nihilistic war on decency and truth. But we must start with the dark materials, the labour of the negative, if we are to get there.

JAIRUS BANAJI

Russian Capitalism Today: A Case of 'Primacy of Politics'?

The economic regime that has emerged in Russia since the Soviet dissolution and the resurgence of private capital in the 1990s has received a wide variety of characterisations and labels; from 'state capitalism' (which includes various versions, such as Catherine Belton's 'hybrid KGB form of state capitalism'), to Karen Dawisha's 'authoritarian kleptocracy', Richard Sakwa's 'managed capitalism', and, of course, 'crony capitalism', which is now widely used. My own preference would be 'Kremlin-controlled capitalism'.

I want to take a different approach here. Instead of obsessing about the proper terms to use for the capitalist system in Russia, what I want to do is try and get some sense of its peculiarities. Putin's reassertion of control over the oil and gas industry would have meant little had the global oil market not seen a steady resurgence, with crude prices more than tripling in real terms between 2000 and 2008. The oil boom injected huge sums into the Russian economy and, as Chris Miller has argued, radically reshaped Russian politics. Khodorkovsky's Yukos had become Russia's leading oil producer by 2002. When Putin had him arrested in October 2003, ostensibly on tax evasion charges that would have applied with as much force to Abramovich, the issue of how much the oligarchs inherited from Yeltsin's regime would continue to exercise disproportionate influence on government was decisively settled. Media barons were driven out of the country, Khodorkovsky and other Yukos executives jailed for long sentences, and the rest of the Yeltsin-era oligarchs brought rapidly into submission. Meanwhile, the state's oil tax revenues grew by a factor of almost fifteen by the middle of the decade, to over $80 billion. But oil prices collapsed at the end of 2008 and the sizeable budget surpluses of earlier years evaporated. A second crash in the middle of 2014 lasted for well over two years, 'low oil prices ravaging all of Russia's key economic indicators'. (The calculation is that for every fall of $10 in the price of Urals crude, Russia's GDP declines by 1 per cent.)

If one had to periodise Putin's rule, the easiest economic breakpoint would be around 2008. After that year, things became considerably bleaker, especially from 2014. It was clear that Putin had no strategy for restarting growth. Both of the major military assaults on Ukraine have occurred against this background of economic stagnation. But a key development of this phase in politics was the emergence of a new grassroots opposition at the end of 2011, against the backdrop of a massively rigged Duma election.

At the theoretical level, I can think of at least three frameworks from earlier historical periods that would count as candidates for explaining the nature of Russian capitalism over the last two or three decades. For convenience, these can be called: Integrationism; Sectors of Capital; and the Primacy of Politics. They aren't incompatible, of course, because in large part they capture different aspects of what we are trying to explain or characterise. Integrationism first surfaced in a major way in the Soviet economic debates of the 1920s and was essentially the position Trotsky took from 1925 – in contrast not just to Bukharin and others but also to Preobrazhensky, as Richard Day showed in his classic study, *Leon Trotsky and the Politics of Economic Isolation*. Trotsky believed it was impossible for the nascent Soviet state to industralise without drawing on the resources of the world economy.

Integrationism resurfaced strongly in Stephen Hymer's work on international companies and what is distinctive about them, and was incorporated into Bob Rowthorn's stimulating piece on the issue of imperialism in *New Left Review* in 1971. Hymer's conception was that the integration of world economy was being driven by a cross-penetration of domestic markets by the biggest firms in America, Europe and Japan. Rowthorn asked which model of imperialism best described its likely nature in the decade that had just begun, describing these respectively as 'superimperial-ism', 'ultra-imperialism' and 'imperial rivalry'. Hymer's work fits best with the ultra-imperialism model, since it foregrounded the growing mobility and integration of capital against either over-whelming US dominance or conflict-ridden rivalry between firms and their respective national states. In other words, economic inte-gration across national boundaries presupposes peaceful relations between capitalist states.

The second framework, 'Sectors of Capital', is an approach that partly derives from Hilferding in the 1920s when he drew a sharp contrast between firms in German chemicals and electrical engi-neering, and others in heavy industry, to surmise that the earlier dominance of the steel and mining industries was more or less over. This perspective shapes Alfred Sohn-Rethel's analysis of the divisions within German capital from the economic revival of the mid-twenties down to the depression and Hitler's seizure of power in 1933, and how these played out politically. In *Economy and Class Structure of German Fascism*, he shows that heavy industry was the backbone of the Harzburg Front, the informal coalition that leaned furthest to an authoritarian solution. I G Farben, a major German chemical and pharmaceutical conglomerate, by contrast, was the last major enterprise to extend formal submission to the Nazi state.

The last of our frameworks, 'Primacy of Politics', is a concept borrowed from Tim Mason, the exceptionally creative Marxist historian of Nazi Germany who, tragically, died by suicide in 1990. He first articulated this view in the West German periodical *Das*

Argument in 1966. Reviewing Mason's argument in 1970, Peter Sedgwick summed up its essential thesis by saying that National Socialism displayed a 'primacy of politics' in which ideological goals determined 'the performance of the economic sphere so radically that the whole system cuts loose from any rationality of self-reproduction'. Mason himself traced this self-destructive, irrational mode of capitalist governance back to the disintegration of capital as a collective force – that is, as a class that was coherent and cohesive enough to determine at least those aspects of state policy that affected accumulation directly or indirectly. As he said, 'the direct links between the economic and political elites became weaker than they had been in the Weimar Republic'. In Mason's essay the chief takeaway is that under capitalism '*there is always something irrational about the assertion of a primacy of politics*'. Irrationality is the underlying theme.

Each of these frameworks can be helpful in explaining contemporary Russia. The global expansion of Russia's energy giants illustrates a purely integrationist logic, since profitability in the oil and gas sector is driven by an expanding presence in world markets. In her essay for *Journal of International Affairs*, Poussenkova has shown this for firms like Gazprom and Rosneft. Here there is no question of imperialist rivalry in the traditional Marxist sense, since expansion involves both a greater integration of world economy as well as extensive collaboration between firms of different nationalities. Rosneft's international alliances with firms like BP (for Kara Sea) and ExxonMobil (for Sakhalin-I) are good examples of this.

The second aspect, sectors of capital, is useful in explaining the major shift that occurred in the balance of power between private capital and the state as Putin promoted state corporations and recovered control of the oil and gas industry against the earlier dominance of the oligarchs. But the oligarchs or billionaires themselves were not a static group. The most powerful of them, Khodorkovsky, was destroyed by Putin after he was arrested and jailed in the mid 2000s, while Rem Vyakhirev – who ran Gazprom 'as if it were his personal fiefdom' – was shunted out even earlier, in 2001. On the other hand, many more billionaires would emerge in

Russia in the 2000s, and while the global financial crash destroyed many of those fortunes, especially in banking, the bulk of this class of capitalists could show a more diversified economic base by 2015, compared to the assets they owned in 2005. The earliest oligarchs had built their fortunes in hydrocarbons, metals and banking, largely through rigged auctions. By 2015, however, real estate, trade, chemicals and telecom had all emerged as newer sectors of capital accumulation, while in the gas market independent producers linked to powerful oligarchs began to eat into Gazprom's market share. Most large private-sector firms in Russia are run by dominant shareholders who use offshore companies to bolster their control. The late 1990s and early 2000s saw staggering levels of hostile takeovers, which were simply coerced, or violent seizures of capital assets that made up a corporate raiding industry in which state officials and businessmen worked closely together. It was estimated that in Moscow alone in the first half of 2005 there were seventy violent business takeovers.

Primacy of politics can be illustrated by Chris Miller's assertion that those oil and gas magnates who retained ownership of their energy assets did so by 'ensuring that they satisfy the Kremlin's political goals before pursuing their own financial self-interest'. This is an extraordinary feature of any capitalism, since accumulation is subordinated to the needs of the state. This, of course, was part of Putin's vision, which was summed up in an official document in 2003 which said 'the role of the country in the global energy markets largely determines its geopolitical influence'. Here it is impossible to separate the state's political ambitions from the strategic economic decisions that are made by the oil and gas majors. Or, to take an example that is particularly relevant now, a *Reuters* investigation into Russian customs documents revealed that Gazprom 'sold more than 20 billion cubic metres of gas well below market prices' to one Dmitry Firtash, a Ukrainian oligarch with close ties to the Kremlin, in the four years leading up to 2014. 'The price Firtash paid was so low,' *Reuters* calculates, 'that companies he controlled made more than $3 billion on the arrangement'. Other documents revealed that 'bankers close to Putin granted Firtash credit lines of up to $11 billion … to buy a dominant position in [Ukraine's] chemical and fertiliser industry and expand his influence'. Firtash was a major financial backer of Yanukovich. The general point to emerge from this investigation was simply that 'Putin uses Russian state assets to create streams of cash for political allies', converting Gazprom into a tool of Russian foreign policy. (In the early 2010s there was a sharp reduction in Ukraine's consumption of Russian gas, so that by 2016 the European Union was supplying more gas to Ukraine than Russia was.)

To step back for a moment, between Gorbachev and the first shoots of a Russian spring and the stormclouds of the Second Chechen War that ushered in Putin's own regime lay the catastrophic 1990s when state enterprises were sold for absurdly small sums as part of Chubais' voucher-privatisation scheme. This was followed by a later scheme known as loans-for-shares, resulting in Russia's industrial wealth being auctioned off at ridiculously low prices, as if an undervaluation of capital was one more lever of primitive accumulation to be added to Marx's list in volume one of *Capital*. State-owned equity stakes worth $14 billion were sold to the oligarchs for less than $1 billion. Two particularly striking examples illustrate this contrived undervaluation: Khordorkovsky's acquisition of Yukos, and the sale of Gazprom. Yukos was valued at $350 million 'though it would have a market cap of $6.2 billion eight months later'! While the implicit price of Gazprom in the auctions was $250 million when the company's market cap would have been worth anywhere between $300 and $700 billion in terms of gas reserves alone! These privatisation schemes were tantamount to theft, but it was theft that reflected both the corrupt and predatory nature of Russia's experiment with private capitalism (encouraged by the West) as well as the shambolic character of Yeltsin's own regime, which was rife with criminality and consumed by the 'pervasive corruption and incompetence' that Paul Klebnikov exposed in his book *Godfather of the Kremlin*.

The spree of mismanagement that allowed for such large-scale siphoning of state resources brought the economy to the brink of bankruptcy by the later 1990s, since the state had effectively given away the most profitable parts of Russian industry and forfeited its major source of revenue. At this level, Putin set out to reverse the relationship between state and capital by recentralising the state (not least against the hold of regional governors), consolidating the state's command over business and enormously tightening his own grip over its various apparatuses, especially the security services that he himself sprang from. A key difference between Yeltsin's regime and the one that followed is that Putin broke the political power of the oligarchs. This had two immediate implications. In the first place, it allowed for a new set of oligarchs to emerge and those who did never dreamed of challenging Putin's authority. It also allowed the government to re-establish control over decisive economic sectors that had been usurped under Yeltsin.

However, nothing could be more misleading than to identify the twenty-odd years that Putin has been in power with a simple reassertion of state capitalism in some generic sense of this term. This is where the challenge for theory lies. For example, in *Putinom- ics,* Chris Miller refers to 'oligarch-dominated state-owned firms in energy and other key sectors', which shows that state capitalism *per se* cannot be a sufficiently accurate description of the complex ways in which the private power of capital is articulated under Putin. To take the most striking case of this, the state corporations created by Putin are widely regarded as corrupt and badly managed. Thus 'close associates of Putin run the biggest state companies, and they are responsible only to him'. Igor Sechin at Rosneft and Vladimir Yakunin at Russian Railways are good examples of these public-sector chief executives who treat state-owned companies almost as if they were their private property.

Beyond them lies a charmed circle of businessmen who are old personal friends of Putin's from his St Petersburg days. They are said to have 'become billionaires through preferential deals with the Russian government, mainly by receiving large no-bid procure- ment orders from Gazprom and by buying Gazprom assets cheaply'. Thus the only construction firms building gas pipelines for Gazprom are both owned by close friends of Putin who are members of his 'inner circle'. The Rotenberg brothers – Arkady and Boris, who are described as Putin's judo buddies – on the one hand, and Gennady Timchenko on the other. The Rotenbergs are said to 'have made billions of dollars in contracts for Gazprom', outside any competitive bidding process, and Gazprom is said to overinvest in pipelines that are not 'commercially viable'. The Sochi Winter Olympics was another project awarded to them, with Navalny's foundation documenting numerous instances of corruption related to the Sochi construction projects. The massive bridge linking Crimea to Russia, the Kerch Bridge, is also one of Arkady Rotenberg's projects, a multibillion dollar contract he won in 2015. Putin drove a Kamaz truck across the bridge as part of its official opening in May 2018. As for Timchenko, the other big supplier of gas pipelines and, oddly enough, a sponsor of the St Petersburg judo club where Putin trained as a young man: his net worth is estimated to be $22 billion, which makes him the sixth richest Russian billionaire on the 2021 Forbes list. In an extraordinary intervention, when the EU sanctioned Timchenko in April 2014, Putin rushed to his defense by complaining publicly of a 'flagrant violation of human rights' – a rare concern for Putin – because the sanctions had frozen his wife's bank account and credit cards and made it impossible for her to pay for surgery that she urgently needed. In Moscow, Timchenko lives in 'one of the grand old Stalinist Politburo villas on the Sparrow Hills overlooking the capital'.

Of course, the power elite that Putin has built around himself is more complex than just his closest friends (Igor Sechin, the Arkady brothers and so on) and starts with an inner circle of former KGB friends who have successfully seized control of the FSB, other security agencies and the state apparatus more widely. And, as the former Swedish diplomat Åslund argues in his book, *Russia's Crony Capitalism*, at the other end of the financial flows that start with the corrupt management of both state and private enterprises are the bankers and authorities in offshore tax havens in the West who collude in laundering money for Putin's various concentric circles. The sheer scale of Russia's flight capital (well over a trillion dollars on some estimates) makes kleptocracy an essential dimension of Russia's capitalism, and as with countries such as India, for example, it would be impossible to study the way big business is structured and the way it functions without making this dimension pivotal to the nature of these economies. By definition, of course, flight capital reduces the mass of surplus value available for accumulation domestically, and thus feeds into stagnation. Going after the offshore accounts of Russia's oligarchs would mean prising open entire circuits of capital flight and capital circulation implicating other countries as well as the banking systems of the West, and we can be sure that this is not the kind of counterattack Biden or anyone else is ever likely to contemplate by way of sanctions. Putin himself holds tens of billions of dollars of assets abroad and was visibly upset by the publication of the Panama Papers, according to Obermayer and Obermaier in *The Panama Papers*. Åslund guesses that he's probably transferred anywhere between $100 to $160 billion into offshore accounts since 2006, which is less than Browder's estimate of $200 billion.

If Putin's oligarchs made their fortunes from the state then, far from implying the sort of rivalry between state and private capital that dominated India's industrial expansion in the fifties, this suggests a symbiosis between two leading sectors of Russian capital – the new oligarchs on one side and the various state corporations in energy, transport, banking and arms production that were specially created by Putin, on the other. In her book *Putin's Kleptocracy*, Karen Dawisha argues that when he came to power 'Putin wanted the oligarchs to understand that they would have rents from these companies [meaning the extractive industries at the commanding heights of the economy] only as a reward for loyal state service. *But for an oligarch loyal to Putin there would be no restrictions on the profits that could be realised*'. This captures the deal perfectly and also explains why such formidable fortunes have been made and siphoned off in an incredibly short span of time. Loyalty meant that the oligarchs would have to stay out of opposition politics, which almost invokes Trotsky's image of the still-born character of Russian liberalism and the defunct nature of Russia's bourgeoisie.

Anders Åslund's recent book *Russia's Crony Capitalism* frames Russian capitalism entirely through the prism of Putin's inner circle and the corrupt deals that have enriched them, largely at the expense of minority shareholders in listed state firms such as Gazprom which have seen their market cap decline steeply. The distracting feature of this account, welcome as it is, is that it surely cannot be the whole of what Russia's capitalism is about. Scholars like Ilya Matveev have tried to project a more independent role for Russian big business by underscoring the kind of corporatist bargaining that goes on between the ministries and the key business associations. For example, presidential economic adviser Andrei Belousov recently proposed creating a special tax that would skim the 'excess profits' of the biggest exporters outside oil and gas – profits that he attributed to the devaluation of the ruble and high natural resource prices on the global market – saying it would yield half a trillion rubles in fresh tax revenues. In response, the Russian Union of Industrialists and Entrepreneurs (RUIE), the leading business association, objected that it would simply lead to a 'mass exodus of investors from the Russian market' and the proposal was dropped. Concentrating on the so-called cronies throws little light on the mass of Russian big business, where the interesting issues are who the capitalists are, which economic sectors they represent, how competitive their firms are in international markets, and how they deal with workers, unions and consumers.

One very rough way of starting to examine these more complex questions is to see who Russia's leading billionaires are today. In *Forbes'* latest list of the top ten billionaires, Timchenko and Alisher Usmanov, Russia's largest iron ore producer, are the only capitalists who can really be said to have close personal ties to Putin. Pavel Durov, who created the messaging app Telegram in 2013, is the only high-tech entrepreneur in the list, while the rest are all connected with steel or with mining of one kind or another, except Vagit Alekperov, head of Lukoil, Russia's second-largest oil company. The richest businessman in the top ten is Alexey Mordashov, a steel magnate and chief executive of Russia's largest steel and mining company Severstal. What's interesting about Mordashov is the way he reacted to his recent inclusion in the EU sanctions list. According to one news report, 'describing himself as being removed from politics, he called for an end to Russia's war in Ukraine which he called a "tragedy of two fraternal peoples"'. 'It is terrible that Ukrainians and Russians are dying, people are suffering hardships, the economy is collapsing. We must do everything necessary so that a way out of this conflict is found in the very near future and the bloodshed stopped', he's quoted as saying. The third richest Russian on the *Forbes* list, also a steel tycoon, chairman of the NLMK group, Vladimir Lisin, expressed similar sentiments in March. In a letter to steelworkers, he wrote that the death of people in Ukraine is a 'tragedy it is impossible to justify' and urged Putin to find a peaceful diplomatic solution. The board of directors of Lukoil (whose president Alekperov is the fourth richest on the *Forbes* list) also broke ranks with Putin in issuing a call for an end to the war. These are voices from the very top end of Russian industry and they help to undermine clichéd representations of Russian capital as entirely beholden to Putin.

The Russian steel industry is in fact the one sector of manufacturing that has successfully created several world-class companies, even as the bulk of manufacturing in Russia remains hopelessly uncompetitive by global standards. Steel is a typical oligopoly, with the top five producers accounting for 91 per cent of total production in 2017. If Lisin's company leads this group of steel capitalists, the second largest producer of steel is EVRAZ, a multinational owned by Roman Abramovich which employs some 70,000 people worldwide, 95 per cent of them in Russia. Russian steel also depends crucially on export markets, which doubtless is why industrialists like Mordashov and Lisin are so worried about the impact of sanctions.

The rapid growth of Russia's economy in the years from 1999 to 2008 was sustained by the oil boom and the state's ability to tax a major share of the export revenue from the hydrocarbon sector. Oil and gas contributed 60 per cent of Russian exports by 2005, and almost 40 per cent of the central government's tax receipts. The boom was absolutely crucial in giving Putin what Thane Gustafson in *Wheel of Fortune* calls the 'resources to rebuild the central state's apparatus of coercion and control', but also to stabilising the regime by widening its support base beyond the *siloviki* and his own immediate circles of the men from St Petersburg, the *Pitertsy*. As Simon Pirani has argued in *Change in Putin's Russia*, the rising living standards that came about in those years after their catastrophic decline and the wage repression of the nineties 'were the main source of Putin's popularity'.

But the crisis of 2008 has since ushered in a long period of pressure for the economy, one marked by repeated stagnation, and of course Putin's wars (in Chechnya, Georgia, Syria and Ukraine) – and the sanctions they've provoked when Ukraine was the target – have done nothing to relieve that. The depression was especially bad in the metallurgical regions which are typically characterised by one-company towns where the population depends crucially on a single, often struggling factory and where workers have in the past generally been successful in avoiding closure of the dominant enterprise.

In 2016, some sixty percent of monotown residents were reported as finding their conditions of life unbearable, prompting government to adopt a colour-coded classification of such towns according to the degree of perceived risk in terms of the threat of social explosion. The worst-off mono-towns were described as the 'red hundred'. Being on the monotown list entitles communities to subsidies from the state and Putin has at least been careful to give the impression that he wishes these to continue.

However, it's the large steel companies that have broken this legacy-pattern of firms safeguarding employment; as Stephen Crowley points out, they have begun to cut the number of workers substantially. Many of the workers who are laid off by large companies are often simply reemployed in other enterprises of the company. Alexey Mordashov, owner of Severstal, is quoted as saying, 'I believe there's a sort of social contract in many companies'. Nonetheless, '[i]n 2013, six major steelmakers were said to cut their payrolls by 33,500, reducing employment by over 9 per cent' compared to the previous year.

The Russian car industry was built by attracting foreign capital through import substitution. In 2006, when foreign models began to outsell Russian ones, policy changed and there was a scramble for the Russian car market. Ford, Toyota and Nissan set up factories near St Petersburg, and the leading Russian carmaker Avtovaz was bought by Renault, which invested more than a billion dollars in the project. One of the most fascinating aspects of this influx of foreign capital is its impact on the unions. Quoting again from Crowley's recent book, *Putin's Labor Dilemma*,

> the (new) policy also appeared successful for workers in the automobile sector, where one of the strongest alternative union organisations, the MPRA (Inter-regional Labor Union of Automobile Workers) was formed by workers from two automobile plants (Ford in Vsevolozhsk and AvtoVAZ) in 2006, just as the import substitution policy had begun. The MPRA led some of the most successful labor actions in Russia, such as the 2007 strike at the Ford plant, where workers halted production and barred entry to the plant, and by doing so won wage gains of 11 per cent and a contract guaranteeing wage indexation of 1 per cent above inflation. The Ford contracts became an inspiration for other workers in the industry, and the MPRA spread to other auto plants such as Volkswagen-Kaluga.

By the 2010s, the Russian car market was the second largest in Europe, slightly behind that of Germany, and Crowley notes that

> as the outlook improved, autoworkers again went on the offensive. For example, in March 2012, while the protests against electoral fraud were still taking place in Moscow and St Petersburg, not far from Moscow workers at Benteler Automotive, an auto parts supplier for the Volkswagen plant, undertook a three-day strike that nearly shut down the VW plant, in order to gain recognition of their MPRA affiliated union.

However, the collapse of the oil boom in 2014 again pushed the car industry into a deep crisis, and, of course, the recent sanctions have meant the withdrawal of foreign firms. On the other hand, as the MPRA expanded to cover other industrial sectors and called itself the Inter-Regional Trade Union Workers' Association, the authorities took court action to have the union declared illegal in the run-up to Putin's 2018 reelection campaign, but the Supreme Court has overturned that ruling.

Describing the essential conflict at the heart of Russia's economy requires juxtaposing two of the themes outlined at the start. The conflict discussed above between economics and politics is expressed as a clash between the integrationist logic of capital and the 'primacy of politics' encapsulated in Putin's statism. This conflict was most dramatically expressed in the drive to destroy Khodorkovsky's control of Yukos and absorb the best parts of the company into the state-owned 'national champion' Rosneft which, like Gazprom, was simply a cash-cow for Putin's geopolitical ambitions. The very selection of Igor Sechin as head of Rosneft shows this since he was 'the unofficial leader of the *silovik* wing of the Kremlin elite', as Gustafson describes him, and someone who, like Putin, was part of the KGB cadre in the mid-1980s. Here it's useful to use Sartre's notion of 'incarnation' to get some sense of the importance of figures like Khodorkovsky, Sechin and Putin. Yukos was Russia's largest and most aggressive private-sector oil company, its owner an unabashed defender of a modern, globally integrated capitalism who was increasingly seen in the West as a corporate governance role model. As Catherine Belton says in *Putin's People*,

> of all the Moscow oligarchs, Mikhail Khodorkovsky was the one most actively seeking to integrate his company into the West, most openly courting Western investors and leaders for support. He was leading the way in trying to instil Western corporate governance methods and transparency at his company, after years of being a bad boy of Russia's Darwinian business scene. The conflict that unfolded as Putin's *siloviki* fought to wrest

away Khodorkovsky's control of Yukos's west Siberian oilfields was at once a clash of visions for Russia's future, and a battle for empire. It was to define Russia's imperial resurgence and Putin's efforts to restore his country as an independent force against the West. But it was also a clash that was deeply personal.

It is perfectly obvious that Putin and Khodorkovsky detested each other not in some purely personal sense but for what each represented to the other. Khodorkovsky was outspoken to the point of arrogance, often attacked the state officials in the media, and was not easily beaten into submission even when the attempt came from Putin. Belton reports that '[h]e was pouring tens of millions of dollars into funding the Communists' and that two of the top executives from Yukos 'headed the Communist Party candidates list'. His funding of opposition parties in the Duma clearly rankled Putin. It is reported that at a private dinner in May 2003 to which Khodorkovsky and Abramovich were asked to come, Putin ordered Khodorkovsky to 'stop funding the Communists', but he is said to have flatly refused, apparently saying that 'the support of democracy in Russia was just as important as the business'. In July that year, Putin told the prime minister Mikhail Kasyanov that 'Khodorkovsky had crossed a line by financing the Communists without his permission'.

In his brilliant book on the Russian oil industry, *Wheel of Fortune*, Thane Gustafson has a long and vivid description of the various issues over which Putin and the oil executive had fiercely opposed views and clashed publicly. These included a pipeline to China that Yukos was strongly in favor of, against Putin's idea of a line that would extend thousands of miles further directly to the Pacific Coast – an idea that Khodorkovsky publicly mocked. And then there was the plan of merging Yukos with Chevron to create the world's largest oil company.

Given the role of institutional investors in world capitalism today, no business can hope to access capital markets internationally unless it complies with benchmark disclosure standards and levels of transparency that make minority shareholders (that is, the financial institutions) and international creditors 'comfortable'. It has been said (in Khodorkovsky's case), 'one wonders if a little less transparency might not have been wiser'. By contrast, the governance structures of the state companies and corporations are far removed from anything that would be remotely acceptable in terms of international best practice. Thus the boards of the state corporations and companies are appointed by Putin, their chief executives are his men, answerable only to him, so that even state, that is, public control is a legal fiction. In Gazprom's case this sort of governance culture has led to what one writer describes as 'seventeen years of disastrous management', while Yakunin's control of Russian Railways in the years 2005-15 reeked of corruption, Navalny making him a prime target of his exposés. The sprawling defense conglomerate Rostec was the creation of Sergei Chemezov, who's been friends with Putin since their KGB days in East Germany. As one critic has written,

> Rostec doesn't publish any financial reports, annual reports, or other detailed information about its business. This vast business empire of often secret companies is a nontransparent maze ... it abandoned its website in English in 2018 ... [However,] Rostec makes one thing clear, its dependence on the president: 'The Rostec Corporation is governed by its supervisory group, executive board, and general director, who is appointed by the President of the Russian Federation.'

But the wider issue here is which pattern capitalism evolves by – in other words, either the state services capital accumulation (this is, if you like, the standard pattern linked to liberal democracies that are dominated by powerful corporate interests), or accumulation services the state (this is the non-standard, statist-authoritarian pattern reminiscent of what Tim Mason called 'the primacy of politics' and is exemplified as much by the Saudis under Mohammed bin Salman as by Russia under Putin).

There are of course different senses of the expression 'primacy of politics', some stronger than others. For example, when one writer states that '[g]overnment-owned firms are managed with political goals in mind', that is one obvious but weaker sense of the term. It introduces a radical heteronomy into the heart of the accumulation process, since some of the largest firms are restrained from functioning as purely capitalist enterprises. However, there is a much stronger sense of primacy that is strikingly evident in the wars Putin has waged both in Syria and in Ukraine. For example, when Russian troops annexed Crimea, this was the result of a decision that Putin could not have shared more widely than with a narrow circle. It is clear that the ministry of finance hadn't been consulted. The Deputy Finance Minister Tatyana Nesterenko claimed at the time, '[t]he Ministry of Finance was not asked in advance about the possible price of the decision on the accession of Crimea'.

And, of course, the massive sanctions that have now swept over Russia will do major damage to the economy and the lives of its population, not to mention the world economy which now faces the prospect of a recession that will last for years, given that Russia is the world's largest exporter of commodities, not just oil and gas but, for example, titanium, which is vital to the world's aerospace industries. Thus Putin's wars undermine the interests of big capital as a whole, as Ilya Matveev noted with respect to the first invasion of Ukraine and its impact on Russian business. The question is: does Putin care? The last few years have seen an erosion of the 'Putin majority', as Budraitskis calls it, and this could well be one factor in the decision to unleash war on Ukraine. But as the war machine is mobilised, so is the machinery of repression, which means even worse authoritarianism than most ordinary Russians have seen in the period since 2011.

If the minority liberal sector of Russian capital failed spectacularly in its confrontation with Putin, what about the working class? As oil and gas production replaced coal as the backbone of Russia's economy, this weakened the structural position of industrial workers, Stephen Crowley argues in his book *Putin's Labor Dilemma*. Like working classes worldwide, it has to build more powerful union organisations before it can start flexing political muscle, but it's worth noting that in Belarus, in the mass demonstrations of 2020, workers formed strike committees in leading state-owned enterprises and were a conspicuous part of the movement against Lukashenko, with demands denouncing his rigging of elections and police brutality. This was Lukashenko's 'traditional constituency' rising up against him and he was visibly shocked. The lesson here is that workers acted as part of a wider mass struggle for democracy, as indeed they did in Egypt in 2011. So that leaves the Russian grassroots opposition which has partly coalesced around Navalny. The fate of the war in Ukraine will be crucial to Putin's future. It has shown most sectors of Russian society – which don't buy into the Kremlin's absurd propaganda about Russia's territorial integrity being under threat – the sheer irrationality and almost genocidal brutality the regime is capable of in order to perpetuate the political lifespan of its president and of the corrupt circles that have the greatest stake in his continued rule.

All that said, if one is looking for a purely economic explanation of why Putin has invaded Ukraine twice in the past eight years, consider the fact reported by Rupert Russell in his book *Price Wars*:

> In 2012, enormous gas reserves – 2.3 trillion cubic metres – were discovered under Ukraine's share of the Black Sea. Russia tried to negotiate access to the deposits, but the talks fell through. Then in January 2013, Ukraine struck a deal with Royal Dutch Shell to start drilling in Eastern Ukraine, where another major deposit of natural gas had been discovered.

So much so that the Ukrainian energy minister apparently said that 'Ukraine would become a net exporter to Europe – competing with Russia – by 2020'.

ERIC BLANC

(Re)Organising the Private Sector: Amazon, Starbucks, and a Revitalised Labour Movement?

This conversation took place in January 2023.

Salvage: We were hoping that you could set the scene a little by talking about the recent breakthroughs and ongoing organising campaigns in the American labour movement that you've been following and why you think they're so significant.

Eric Blanc: Sure. It's a contradictory situation because on the one hand, this is the most exciting time for new union organising that I've seen in my lifetime, and there's a tremendous amount of interest and momentum from below. On the other hand, the actual number of workers who have unionised and gone on strike – and, even more so, won new contracts – is actually still at a relative historic low. It's higher than in previous years, but that's because things really bottomed out.

So the dynamic on the positive side is that there's been a tremendous increase in new union organising at some key corporations that have long been considered really unorganisable (at least under the current anti-union legal conditions in the US).

The biggest wins for workers in the US over the last year have been at Starbucks, where over 300 stores have voted and won a union, and at Amazon where workers in Staten Island in New York successfully voted to unionise. Those two drives in particular really captured a lot of attention. One of the key dynamics that we've seen this past year is the way that working people over social media, through their personal connections, see these wins and then try to replicate them at their own workplaces. I think that's an exciting dynamic, and one of the most novel aspects of what's going on.

You have this contagion, this attempt to really replicate successes by workers from below taking the initiative on their own to unite their workplaces. We've seen workers at Chipotle, Apple, Google, Home Depot, Trader Joes, REI, and in a variety of different significant corporations take these initiatives to unionise – and most of the time these were workers initiating things on their own, young workers, supporters of Bernie Sanders and Black Lives Matter, who have been pushed out of economic opportunities and who have frequently taken the lead with little or minimal union support.

There are other drives as well that reflect more longstanding dynamics. We've seen a lot of unionisation efforts in higher education and publishing, for instance. There's been a continued fight back amongst nurses. But I think the newest thing is this worker-to-worker organising, in which you have either independent unions – like at Amazon – or hybrid efforts, where there is some union support and where unions are providing resources, but the day to day work is mostly worker-to-worker, rather than staff-to-worker. This is what's most emblematic at Starbucks, but also in the really tremendous increase in unionisation in journalism and the work of the NewsGuild, which parallels Starbucks in its worker-to-worker, but union supported, efforts.

Can you talk a little bit more about that dynamic where these things are not initiated by the existing unions? Specifically, can you speak to where these worker-leaders have been drawing their inspiration and experience from? You mentioned the Sanders campaign in passing and we'd love to hear what you think about the role that played in shaping the current upsurge, and also whether you think earlier upticks in strike activity – like the Red State rebellions among teachers you have written about – have played a role in the confidence on display in the past year.

The way I look at it is that there are some conjunctural factors that have led to this dynamic and then there are some more long-term factors that are likely to continue, irrespective of what happens to this current uptick in labour.

Some of the conjunction of factors are obviously the pandemic, a tight labour market, and also a favourable National Labor Relations Board, which has played a significant role in allowing some of these drives to spread and scale up. The deeper, more long-term factors I see are – on the basis of outrageous levels of economic inequality – first, the crystallisation of a young layer of radical workers over the last few years. In the interviews I've done these people point to a variety of experiences from Black Lives Matter to gun control to Roe v Wade, but the thing that pops up most frequently is the Bernie Sanders campaign. In part because that campaign, I think, articulated a sense of class struggle and an overall frame of 'the enemy are the billionaires and the solution is the collective action of working people'.

It was easy for people who got excited about Bernie and then maybe got their first volunteer experience there to transition to thinking, 'well, you know, we lost in the electoral arena, but the fight continues, I'm going to try to take on Jeff Bezos, or to take on Howard Schultz [the CEOs of Amazon and Starbucks, respectively], I'm going to take them on at work'.

And one of the moving aspects of the uptick that I've seen is a sense that all hope is not lost. There's a prevailing doomerism these days, having to do with the rise of climate disaster and the incipient authoritarianism from the Republicans, and these labour struggles have been a real source of hope.

One of the nice things about the workplace is that it's a place where you can organise without having to wait for anybody from above. It feels like – and this is something that workers told me over and over – 'I saw they can do it', in reference to Starbucks or Amazon, people feel: 'I saw they could do it and I realised I could do that too'. That is the most unique and I think potentially explosive dynamics in play right now. This copycat factor in which young, radicalised workers have taken the initiative and seen other workers taking initiative. We saw the same dynamics in 2018, when illegal teachers' strikes spread.

There's a second, underlying, deeper cause to the very unique dynamics of these worker-initiated, worker-to-worker efforts, which is the rise of digital technologies. It's very hard to imagine the specific forms that this unionisation uptick has taken without digital technologies which have really dramatically lowered the cost of communication and organisation. So, you have things that would have been unimaginable even a few years ago, like having nationwide trainings where workers share their experiences at Starbucks with other workers. And digital tools made it possible for the Amazon Labor Union – an independent union with little outside backing – to make viral videos, that then in turn raised hundreds of thousands of dollars through GoFundMe to finance their efforts to organise locally.

It would be a mistake to exaggerate the role of digital technologies, to assume they somehow change everything. In many ways organising methods themselves have remained largely the same best practices of good labour organising that have existed for years. Emphasising worker-to-worker outreach while making a list of your co-workers, building strong organising committees, inoculation, and all the rest of the basics. But digital tools have allowed workers to take the initiative and to coordinate without having to rely as much on established unions or union staffers, and it has made it easier for struggles to diffuse.

But the limitations of this drive also point to the need for combining this kind of worker-initiated organising with significant resources, particularly: funds, experienced organisers, and lawyers. These recent unionisation efforts have also come up against ruthless corporate opposition; mass firings, which we can talk about more, point to the need for combining the bottom up approach they enable with the resources of the established unions.

Can you give us some more detail on the point you're making about how these initiatives get generalised? On the one hand, it absolutely seems true, as you're saying, that a big part is workers seeing what's happening and trying things out themselves. But is there also a conscious attempt, even if modest, to do organising trainings or the like? If so, where is that happening, and are those old school means of building confidence and capacities having a measurable impact? Or is it largely this mimetic process you've pointed to?

Well, it really depends on which drive you're talking about. If we look at Starbucks, which has really been the most successful effort this last year, they didn't expect their win in Buffalo in late 2021 to spark a national campaign.

That being said, they were hoping to scale up in their region, and they had an ethos of orienting to young radical workers and from the beginning intended to spread the organising, to not just have it be a one off. Fortunately, they reacted in a way a lot of unions don't: when they saw there was a lot of interest immediately following the win in Buffalo they said 'let's do it'.

And they let workers run with it, instead of spending a year to hire more staff and map out a whole campaign – by which time the momentum could have been lost. Workers from Buffalo began replying to and coaching the other workers across the country who reached out online. That allowed for a very rapid spread of the movement within weeks of the initial success.

So it's both this unexpected interest from workers across the country and, in the Starbucks case at least, a conscious effort to build digitally enabled structures to help it spread as quickly as possible.

The dynamic in the journalism world is very similar. The News-Guild similarly has built worker-to-worker structures through which big wins can then translate into excitement, which in turn translates into mass national trainings. Their member organising program lets union members take over what used to be almost exclusively staff responsibilities for training and mentoring new shops, and lean into using digital technologies to help make this a nationwide movement.

The unfortunate aspect is that these examples are still the exceptions.

I think that it's possible to imagine things having gone further in a lot of different industries – and even at Starbucks and Amazon – if the big national unions (which in the US are confusingly called international unions) with their enormous national structures and significant resources had really risen to the occasion.

There's a confluence of factors that have created a historic opening: support for unions is the highest it's been since the 1960s; the pandemic; the tight labour market; increasingly radicalised young workers; the momentum from a string of exciting victories. Unions for the most part have not seized the moment. They haven't dedicated the type of resources that would be needed to help the large number of workers who are looking to organise their work-places right now.

One of the few exceptions has been Workers United, which has supported the Starbucks campaign. Another major exception is the United Electrical Workers union (UE), which at the start of the pan-demic, along with the Democratic Socialists of America (DSA) and a network of folks who had been involved in the labour organising side of the Bernie Sanders campaign, co-founded the Emergency Workplace Organizing Committee (EWOC). EWOC was explicitly founded to support the type of worker-initiated efforts I've been emphasising in this interview.

It's a structure intended to connect any worker in the country who wants help organising with an experienced labour organiser using the distributed organising tools that the Bernie campaign established – they just fill out a short form online, and within forty-eight hours an organiser will get in touch with them. As a whole, EWOC has proven much more successful than we dreamed.

One of the things that has made me particularly hopeful about EWOC becoming a model, and not just a one-off, is seeing that it has spread to the UK through Organise Now!, which is doing essentially the same type of organising work to support new workers organising. This gives me hope that there is now the possibility of finding new ways to support worker-initiated efforts that may not have been possible in the past. Particularly when you have unions and radicals working together on these types of initiatives.

And you can imagine how the overall course of this movement would change if every union, for instance, was putting real resources towards scaling up today's new organising efforts. But that's not the situation we're currently in.

Your point about the lack of interest in committing resources to these new drives seems like it's worth exploring a little. As you've mentioned in a recent article, this isn't a matter of the money not being there. US unions are sitting on something like $35 billion. Why do you think they're not interested in investing it in the way you're describing? Why are they so stuck in their ways?

There's a rational core to this, which is that organising a union in the United States under the current legal setup is extremely risky and very, very difficult. The reality is that there are very few penalties for employers breaking the law, and for firing workers, and for doing all sorts of things that make union organising difficult. A lot of unions believe that, until there is labour law reform, it's going to be next to impossible to make serious organising inroads.

And so that explains in large part the defensive focus of a lot of unions. There are unions doing good organising locally, but it's nothing at scale, and nothing that would approximate what's appropriate for this moment.

So, in part, I'd say they're misreading the way forward. Saying that labour law reform is necessary is accurate, but it begs the question of what it would take to generate the momentum and power sufficient to make that change feasible?

I think there's a reciprocal dynamic between bottom up struggle and legal changes. The problem with most unions is that they're only looking at it from the top down. Top down initiatives can be helpful. I think we've seen this, for example, with the recent changes in the National Labor Relations Board (NLRB).

It's hard to imagine the Starbucks campaign getting off the ground in the first place if the NLRB had not sided with the workers in Buffalo, by allowing them to have their votes on a store-by-store basis. In the past, companies, including Starbucks, have insisted that union elections be held on a citywide basis, which would have made it almost impossible for the Buffalo campaign to win in the first place.

So the changes from above are significant and shouldn't be minimised. But there's just no way you're going to pass major labour law reform in the United States, where corporations hold so much political power and where the Supreme Court will ultimately get to decide on its 'legality', unless you have millions of workers in motion and unless you have mass disruption from below. It won't happen unless we create a situation where the costs of the status quo continuing are higher than those of making significant concessions to working people.

The prevailing union strategy is unrealistic in that it doesn't provide answers for how to build that sort of bottom-up struggle.

And they've seen an endless amount of evidence that their strategy isn't working. The injunctions against the railway workers being just the most recent.

This reflects not just a misreading of the legal situation, but a long-standing subservience to the Democratic Party establishment. And, again, there's a rational core to their approach. The Republicans are awful, and I don't begrudge unions for trying to defeat the Republicans at the polls. But what has labour gotten for the support it consistently gives to the Democrats? With a few notable exceptions, like the recent NLRB victory, on the whole labour's gotten way less than it's given – and way less than it could get if it took a more independent approach towards top Democratic leaders.

For example, we've seen a huge union busting wave this past year with hundreds of worker organisers being illegally fired by Starbucks. These corporations are doing what they always do, trampling over the nominal rights that workers have, and Joe Biden, for the most part, has remained silent. To me that's even worse than what he did with the rail strike, which was terrible. Blatant union busting at Starbucks and Amazon affects all working people because it resolidifies the fear factor, inhibiting organising everywhere and undercutting the movement's momentum. But instead of organising a pressure campaign to demand that Biden take a public stand and serious action to stop this union busting, most unions have refused to confront the Biden administration in even the most limited of ways. Without that pressure from below, we shouldn't expect establishment Democrats to do the right thing – let alone for them to pass major labour reform.

Let's shift a little bit to talk about socialist strategies for the current moment. Socialists who think that rebuilding the American labour movement should be a major priority have opened up a renewed discussion around the rank-and-file strategy and have argued to use it as a guiding approach for current efforts. What does a rank-and-file-based approach look like in the present moment – in contrast to the period in which it was first articulated – given that there isn't an upsurge in rank-and-file self-organisation being consciously built up as an alternative, or counterweight, to a sclerotic union officialdom?

I think the short version is that the last year has vindicated those who argue that the transformation and rebirth of the labour movement is going to come from below rather than from the top. You need resources and experienced staff organisers, but it's clear that where the energy is, and where you can imagine a path forward, comes from workers taking the lead. And that this could result not only in expanding the labour movement, but in dramatically transforming it.

I've mostly been researching and involved in supporting new union organising, but part of the effort at revitalising the movement from below also takes the form of what we see in the Teamsters union, where a long standing opposition caucus (Teamsters for a Democratic Union) was able, in coalition with others, to win leadership and to begin a transformation process that's likely to culminate in a strike this year at UPS. And we've seen the biggest attendance numbers ever at conferences like Labor Notes, which brings together existing union activists to talk about building caucuses and transforming their unions.

But what's new, and what I think caught even some of our union reform forces a little bit by surprise, is the extent of efforts from young workers on their own to build new unions. Figuring out, as radicals, how we orient towards this new uptick, and how we help it scale up as much as possible, is the $64,000 question.

Recent experience doesn't confirm the assumption which undergirded the thinking of some earlier radicals, that first we'll transform the unions and only then, through those transformed unions, we'd be able to organise the rest of the class.

If anything, the worker-initiated efforts at Starbucks, Amazon, and elsewhere have been an inspiration to existing union members and have put a fire under the butts of existing unions, making it easier for members to push their unions forward and to help overcome the longstanding risk aversion and conservatism that continues to plague the established union movement.

Workplace radicals have been at the fore of these efforts – including through salting.

For readers who don't know, salting is when you consciously get a job in certain industries as part of a strategy of organising those shops. Young leftist salts, for instance, played an important role in the Amazon and early Starbucks victories. At Amazon, the win was really an alliance of young Black and Latino workers with communist and socialist salts. And that is a very promising dynamic.

Until recently, the vast majority of efforts by radicals were aimed at transforming existing unions through things like caucuses – culminating in important actions like the 2012 Chicago teachers strike and the 2019 Los Angeles teachers strike. This current wave of organising over the past year has posed new possibilities. The inspiration generated by these campaigns – by taking on some of the biggest corporations in the world – creates an energy that can hopefully sustain itself and that in turn could feed back into existing unions.

In the short term, the most crucial thing for radicals is to figure out ways to do everything possible to help the campaigns at Starbucks, Amazon, REI, and all of these new efforts, to do everything possible to help them win good first contracts – which is even harder than winning a union election.

I think that is the number one priority. This could look like radicals getting jobs in some of these companies. And wherever you work, you can contribute by helping to organise your workplace.

And for everyone else, it's important to organise solidarity locally for any ongoing unionisation efforts. When workers are on strike, or if they're facing retaliation, that solidarity aspect is crucial. It's all hands on deck whenever any of these workers are in struggle. That should be the first priority for radicals.

At the same time, these DIY efforts can only go so far until the existing union movement is prepared to put real resources behind these efforts. This is where radicals and allied progressives who are correctly reading the moment can play a big role in trying to push from within the existing unions to pivot toward new organising in the way that many unions talked about doing twenty years ago, but haven't for the most part done in practice.

The AFL-CIO, at its last convention in 2022, set a goal of organising one million new workers over ten years. That goal would actually represent an overall decline in union density. The main obstacle here – the reason that the organising targets are so low – is the leadership of these national unions, which for the most part are still stuck in decades-old routines; very few of them have really risen to the occasion. Though on a local level almost all of these national unions have locals doing good work, very few of them have seized this moment in a way analogous to how John L. Lewis in the 1930s threw the treasury of the United Mine Workers into supporting the new unionisation efforts of that period. And the UMW didn't just organise people in coal, but also in steel, and other industries.

One of the things that radicals, in particular, bring to the table is an understanding that the fate of existing unions depends on helping working people win as a whole – the fate of an individual union is inseparable from the fortunes of the rest of the class. Solidarity isn't just good morally, it's essential strategically.

Another one of the bigger picture things we should talk about is the fact that it's become increasingly clear the Federal Reserve in the US – supported by the business press – are really concerned about the tight labour market, and see low unemployment figures as the cause of recent upticks in inflation. Some of the more unvarnished perspectives coming from those quarters even argue in favour of provoking a recession to raise unemployment and supposedly combat inflation. What impact will these efforts and scare-mongering have on the current wave of militancy and new organising? And how should radicals in the labour movement respond?

I think you're exactly right that the Federal Reserve and the key players within the capitalist class understand the dangers of a tight labour market, and that they are pushing to move away from it as quickly as possible.

So, the length of the window for this particular labour uptick is unclear to me.

It's entirely possible that ruthless, employer-supported, union-busting that demoralises and scares people, combined with the continued growth of unemployment, could put an end to the current momentum. If anything, this is even more reason to try to seize the moment while it lasts, rather than doing what it seems like a lot of unions are doing: waiting for things to die down. Then they can say, 'see this is why we didn't want to throw everything into new organising. As you can see, it was just a flash in the pan'.

Part of the reason why such a claim is really short-sighted is that whatever organising happens right now will plant the seeds for years and decades to come. If we look at the thirties as an example again, really the thirties were preceded by decades of attempts to organise, which created new layers of organisers in workplaces, who accumulated experience and built relationships, setting the stage for subsequent struggles. I think we're in that type of situation. I don't think it's realistic to expect we're going to unionise, across the board, a lot of these major corporations in the span of the next year or two, but we can certainly start that process now. And we need union help to do that at scale.

And there's an additional factor. Even if we were to accept the labour law reform focus of most unions – even if you think we need to pass something like the PRO Act before we can possibly see any major breakthroughs in new organising – it's so short-sighted to not realise that the best way to get those sorts of policy changes on the agenda is by doing everything possible to back current organising efforts, regardless of their immediate results in terms of winning first contracts. Big national unions should be taking advantage of this moment to expose the actions of these corporations, to expose the broken nature of existing labour law, and to make a national scandal about companies like Starbucks and Amazon brazenly breaking the law and terrorising tens of thousands of low-wage workers.

These corporations are attempting to double down on just ignoring existing law – not just by firing workers and intimidating them, but by denying benefits and wage increases to unionised workers. Starbucks is doing this now – it's literally against laws already on the books, yet they're doing it anyway.

This is awful, but it's also a huge potential political opportunity. We should have union leaders getting arrested at the White House, demanding that the Biden administration use its bully pulpit and federal contracts against illegal union busting. To its credit, the new Biden-appointed NLRB is playing a very positive role, unlike the

rest of the Biden administration, in supporting these new organising efforts. But on its own the NLRB just doesn't have the power to
enforce the law quickly or strongly enough to force companies like
Starbucks to comply.

The only way to change this is to create a national political
scandal about the fact that CEOs like Schultz and Bezos are trampling on the constitutionally protected rights of workers. To win
big, we need 'the labour question' to return to the centre of political
life – and that requires that unions start acting very differently.

NISHA KAPOOR

A Brave New World: Notes on Citizenship for the Data-State

Despite efforts to the contrary, the recent Nationality and Borders Bill passed into legislation included – among other draconian measures – a quietly added clause enabling the Home Secretary to deprive citizenship without notice. Its enactment contrasted the thwarted efforts to introduce vaccine passports – which attempted to reintroduce the biometric ID in rebranded biosecurity form. Yet both measures indicate changes in state approaches to population management through which norms and protocols of bordering and citizenship are being remade.

Opposition to each has largely proceeded in parallel. Those protesting the former highlighted citizenship as the site of racist politics but granted less attention to the structural and technocratic transformation of the state, of which deprivation is but one part. Those protesting the latter, more concerned with population management than citizenship, drew attention to the punitive nature of the data-state but mostly within a nationalistic, inward-looking framework. In their efforts to mobilise against institutionalised exclusions, both sets of protests illuminate changes to governance that reflect the transformation of the British state over the last twenty years; a transformation in which the authoritarianisms of the racially-charged security state – nurtured in the police, military and border control – have been matched by the authoritarianisms of data governance.

Citizenships, in this context, are frequently treated by capitalist states less as liberal rights-bearing entities and more as commodities open for technocratic cultivation. While powers to remove citizenship will likely be of growing importance as climate catastrophe triggers scarcity and reduces habitable land, it is via the technocracy of e-governance – through which the digitised data-state re-forms subjectivities, administers mass surveillance and promotes conformity and compliance – that a broader spectrum of disenfranchisement is likely to take place. As big tech becomes more enmeshed into the operations of government and the data-state expands, digital identity looks set to be the prism through which bio- and necropolitical drives of the state will be forged.

☭

After 9/11 – in a bid to separate 'genuine refugee' from 'terrorist' – the use of digitised biometrics infiltrated the humanitarian sector and institutionalised the supposition that biometrics could reveal truth. In doing so, biometrics were equipped to assess the veracity of asylum applications, to distinguish between the spurious and the sincere. Via asylum management, biometric identification was rolled out on a global scale as a state governing technology effectively making biometric disclosure a prerequisite for legal recognition. As the security state sought to inscribe papers, or non-papers, onto the body – to momentarily reveal and authenticate – surveillance tech solutions also promised tracking capabilities to scrutinise targets beyond the national border.

Bodily data's linking to behavioural data has been central to the security state's embrace of techno-solutionism, as Evgeny Morozov names it. The data-state is a burgeoning technocracy reliant on digital technologies to connect data dots, find needles in haystacks, ascertain locations, and predict profiles. Scrutiny of biometric identities, security intel, financial records, Driver and Vehicle Licensing Agency (DVLA) histories, civic participation and social standing by automatonic administrators assessing legitimacy, eligibility and overstay – an elaboration of the 'weaponisation of paperwork' that Will Davies speaks of – is growing in sophistication and possibility thanks to its recalibration by digital tech.

The parallel administration of welfare and employment benefits are increasingly reliant on the intelligence of machines to profile, assess and predict, to employ more efficiently and competently the full skill set earlier desired of their human counterparts. So too border policing is hardening because of the employment of technologies designed to construct and fix identity, to make visible the opaque and to relate otherwise discrete data controlled by private and public institutions. Indeed, the hostile environment policy, in its efforts to synthesise population data and promote data sharing between the Home Office and the NHS, education and other state institutions, was as much a test of existing technological capabilities as it was more dog whistle politics. And this trend is only set to worsen, with biosecurity being produced in the image of counterterrorism, intent on delving ever more deeply to mine and extract biodata to make legible 'potentially infectious' populations and to track population movements.

With this push towards technocracy, surveillance tech is also reconstituting the (non)citizen-subject. Over the last twenty years, genetics have merged with behavioural science. Border policing, having routinised biometric data collection, has grown increasingly reliant on the use of prediction profiling, harnessing statistical and technological processes to police 'asylum seekers', 'immigrants', and 'terrorist suspects', not as individuals but by patterns of behaviour and probability – with the effect of casting the 'foreigner' a wider net. Thus, the data-state is interested not only in those who are undocumented, but with all, as Didier Bigo explains, 'who have an action profile that behaviouralists establishing the profiles have judged to be a sign of potential danger'. It is not only that race-class is coded into technical/scientific suppositions as the site of the border is extended, but that one's whole subjecthood is reduced to a series of data nodes where the measure of our worth is restricted to what is knowable and thereby calculable from the AI-derived readings of our biometrics and adjoined digital behaviours.

☭

In a world intent on producing data-subject cyborgs, biometric identification appears a mainstay. It is the foundation of the digital state, to be used not only as a tool for momentary 'authenticatication' but employed as an institutionalised, fixed legal identity. Indeed, India's name for the unique biometric identity granted to residents is *Aadhaar*, meaning 'foundation'. Kenya's Huduma Namba, Swahili for 'service number', is proclaimed by its government to be the 'single source of truth', reinscribing its assigned occultic role for the data-state. Meanwhile, for development capitalists, identification infrastructure is road-building for the digital age. Justifications for the imposition of national digital identification shift in their policing emphasis, generally pivoting between social/welfare management and securitisation. When Britain came its closest to implementing a comprehensive national ID database under Tony Blair's government, it was a combination – border security and the threat of terrorism, welfare and employment – that underpinned policy directives in the name of combatting the threat of opacity, identity fraud and misrepresentation.

Digital identity, now already a multi-billion dollar industry, is projected to exceed $30 billion by 2025, with the number of digital identity apps expected to exceed 6.2 billion by the same year. The issue at hand is no longer whether we can resist digital identity. It is: who will own and manage it, and by doing so, us? Mass digital biometric identities are already here and at the command of the Big Tech sovereigns who, through their 'smart technologies', are thrusting upon us 'smart cities' relying on an amalgam of state cooperation, compliance and cronyism. For the states or sections of them wishing to resist monopolistic Big Tech takeovers, the urge is to construct nation-state equivalents, which governments would control. This was Ursula von der Leyen's reasoning when she suggested the European Commission quickly seek a 'European solution' for vaccine certificates – before Apple or Google got there first.

And as the pandemic hastened surveillance capitalism's opportunity, so it accelerated the urgency for digital data-state futures. The cash cow of crises is the opportunity they provide for ideologically re-framing capitalist imperatives otherwise experiencing friction. Sold to us in the immediate aftermath of the outbreak of Covid-19, the 'screen new deal' – as Naomi Klein phrased it – rebranded and repackaged the all-encroaching tech dystopia encompassing everything from digital classrooms, driverless cars, drone delivery systems, permanent location tracking, and facial recognition-based security systems, many of which, and more, would come together in the beckoned 'smart cities' of the future.

Smart cities promise seamless connectivity and infinite security. AI-driven street sensors, air quality monitors, autonomous buses, self-flying taxis, automated waste sharks and blockchain-based tree planting are already in cultivation, if not in use. As are the public surveillance systems, not least facial recognition cameras, upon which much of the smart city infrastructure depends. These will provide interminable data for fueling preemptive policing systems that will sustain and no doubt worsen the race-classed bordering that already structures urban space. The utopia of the smart city future is to be frictionless, not borderless. All of this, so heavily protested in the months and years prior to the Covid-19 pandemic, could now be better sold and more readily accepted as the key solution to 'pandemic-proofing' our lives, our loves, our livelihoods.

If the seamless, holistic smart city is still in production, the digital biometric surveillance apparatus is implanted and flourishing. Of cities ranked with the most street cameras per person, most of the top ten are in China. Atlanta is tenth. London is sixth. London's Thatcherite legacy of privately installed CCTV cameras installed to police the crises of the 1980s is now a lucrative market opportunity for surveillance firms offering the latest facial recognition technologies to update and advance existing functionality. The police watchlists against which biometric maps of distinct facial points are currently checked by the surveillance systems used by the Metropolitan and South Wales Police will be all the more comprehensive should a national biometric register be made available. A study by professor Pete Fussey of the Met's trial system found it was accurate just 19 per cent of the time; numerous studies in the US have pointed to the racial and gender disparities in accuracy. In India, research concurs, indicating that accuracy of facial recognition software, even when it is produced and tested in the Indian context, is significantly better for men than for women, for lighter skinned Indians than for the darker-skinned.

☭

So how do we make sense of the emerging digital data-state? Emergent designs largely fall under one of two dystopic models. The first simulates itself in the image of the libertarian state – tech style. That is, it uses the foundation of subject datafication – of a digital identity infrastructure – to pursue the creation of digital states, with the aim of realising a market of competing governments. A response to the inadequacies of state governance as the proponents see them, these privately run, private equity–backed 'sovereign-investor' states are to challenge the monopoly that nation-states have over the business of governance, offering the eligible affluent an alternative 'free-market', friction-free digital citizenship, trading and consuming with digital currency. In their predictions for the year 2022, Bernice Lee, research director at the policy think-tank Chatham House, and Ivan Mortimer-Schutts, a senior financial specialist at the World Bank, suggested, albeit somewhat prematurely, that we would enter a world where digital 'countries' would operate alongside nation-states.

Certainly, the flexibility such virtual states are posed to offer, allowing their members to set up legal entities in one country, physically reside in a second, with salaries paid in a third, appear little different from the privileges already enjoyed by the tax-evading citizens of everywhere that the 1 per cent already inhabit. But, with the virtual replication and expansion of such a system, esteemed privileges of pick-and-mix citizenship currently reserved for high-net-worth individuals and offshore companies are set to become available to the next tier down; the 'mass affluent'. And so: the false promise of market inclusivity where – with the assignment of digital identities produced from the calibration of biometrics, property rights, vaccination status – select datizens will be granted access to gated online worlds, including market spaces to, as Lee and Mortimer Schutts continue, 'access digital goods and services that are not licensed or approved in the physical space in which they reside'. These are set to be 'the new offshore, virtual free ports of the digital age.'

Though the virtual state in this form remains in the making, yet-to-be successful libertarian tech efforts to colonise new territories, seas and space in this image are being tried and tested – perhaps the most iconic attempt being the Peter Thiel–backed non-profit Seasteading Institute, which championed the creation of artificial floating nations in international waters. One funded project, Blueseed, aspired to put foreign workers on a cruise ship off the California coast and outside the boundaries of US immigration law – an immigration hack for capital. The inherent contradiction that structures libertarian Silicon Valley – that its desire for minimal government and maximum autonomy operates in conjunction with a business model of state capture capitalism – follows through in these digital floating islands that promise little regulation but monopolistic, secure communications infrastructure. In these gated states, the green-washing of eco-capitalism promises 'sustainability' via energy extraction from the beds of dying seas. While the rest perish.

In the libertarian digital state, sovereignty is to be marketised, citizenship something to be bought and sold. The exclusivity inherent in any such model of statehood, granting frictionless citizenship to those with approving data profiles, accentuates unequal distribution of resources, barring wholesale to the virtual and material wasteland those whose biometrics are immeasurable, or don't measure up.

Running alongside is the second dystopic and currently hegemonic data-state vision – the digital statehood being constructed in the image of the neoliberal nation-state. This model, too, warns against the overreach of government, but in its drive to dissolve the distinction between public and private goods retains neoliberalism's philosophical commitment to – as Sivamohan Valluvan observes – reclaiming the nation as its correct unit, albeit in the image of a market. Protectors of global capital are the central driving force here – the World Bank's programme ID4D, Identity for Development, spearheading the biometric identity rollout currently underway in some form across much of the global south, reliant on loans from the world's largest enabler of transnational capital penetration. Returns to the preoccupation with 'development' are now aimed at servicing tech capitalism, particularly financial technology, where mass establishment of biometric subjecthood is held to be the solution to identity fraud and capitalist imperatives for identity verification. With digital IDs as an indexing device, a whole host of other e-governance initiatives – digitised tax and revenue collections, 'smart' transport management, e-voting and e-billing – proliferate.

Estonia – where World Bank interventions encouraged the creation of a 'digital nation for global citizens' in the early 2000s – is among the most advanced experimenters in this state form. The Estonia model takes seriously the notion of *government as platform*, institutionalised via e-Estonia through which its electronic residents are ascribed a secure identification – enabling access to all manner of social, economic, political and administrative services without ever needing to put foot into the country.

India's digitised nation project took inspiration from this model but upped the ante, scaling up over 1000 times Estonia's efforts so that the project at hand now concerned not a meagre 1.3 million but 1.3 billion residents, making India home to the largest biometric identification system in the world. India Stack, its equivalent e-government project, spearheaded by neoliberal tech personified billionaire and World Bank crony Nandan Nilekani, has established universal biometric identities as the foundation for a data-driven digital economy that has begun with efforts to transform the heavily bureaucratic banking system but desires much beyond. India's model, spurred on by the World Bank–funding Omidyar Network, is in the process of being exported elsewhere – to the Philippines, Sri Lanka, Somalia, Morocco. A comparable and likely compatible system has also been embraced by the UN Refugee Agency (UNHCR), now working with Estonia to roll out digital ID for asylum seekers. Earlier processes of cooperation that saw, for example, the UNHCR pass on refugee identities to state institutions, such as asylum processing institutions in Kenya, may soon function all that much smoother.

Culturally, neoliberal ID proponents frame their efforts in terms of modernisation and efficiency. In India, the effective corporate capitalist assault on the small-scale economic structures that support the poor and working class – which digitisation of the state brings – has gained consensus through a discourse of anti-corruption. Tech-enabled surveillance is promoted as an effective interjection against charlatan middle-men and gangs dealing in distortion – preventing payments and subsidies from reaching their rightful recipients. Anti-corruption narratives serve, no less, the urban middle classes, for whom e-governance epitomises the arrival of the modern techno-financial Indian state, redresses the backwardness of rural regions, and fronts India on the global stage.

In theory, the rewards promise the creation of more and more productive consumer citizens, while improving surveillance and policing capabilities. In reality, digital governance in its current form seems far from the sophisticated, holistic Orwellian nightmare it portends to be. Certainly, population indexing, with its attendant dataset linking, offers tech capital and its various offspun niches possibilities to penetrate untapped markets, to better 'know your customers' – all of which drive a fairly capable surveillance state. But there is also a sense in which digital ID fails to live up to everything it promises. Dysfunctional biometric technologies, the distribution of duplicates, and creation of fraudulent identities are all widely reported in India, making the system more performative than effective. There, inept, clunky, burdensome bureaucracy supplemented by the thuggery of preserved feudal social relations remains core to surveillance and control. Thus the assault implicit in efforts to instil biometric digitisation and widespread digital governance lies – for the disenfranchised labouring classes without internet, without readable fingerprints, without digital literacy, without access to consistent electricity – in the effacement of local systems of accountability, in the policing of human bartering and interaction, and in the hollowing of all avenues through which one's livelihood is fought and sustained. It is via the destruction of such recourses to localised state support that material efficiencies – in the reduction of welfare payments made available to those entitled – are being achieved.

The flipside of such biopolitical drivers are the necropolitical urges mobilised most fervently by authoritarian nationalist forces for whom mass digital surveillance and population indexing offers scientific veneer and sometimes solutionism to the challenges of bureaucracy as a mode of population management. For this camp, data surveillance facilitates the drive to secure those 'edge' populations: unproductive, potentially hostile, and/or simply proclaimed threats against which state nationalisms must rally. In contrast to India's liberal capitalists, such as Nandan Nilekani, for whom digital identity was not to be restricted to citizens but prescribed to all residents in a rather limp effort to disassociate *Aadhaar* from border control, for devout Hindutva nationalists digital identity authentication systems are tools that discern the 'legal' from the 'illegal', that enable the deportation of, in Amit Shah's words, 'infiltrators'. Though objectives differ, with the former promoting development economics and the latter emphasising surveillance, policing and immigration control, it is at this faultline – where the paternal, caretaking state meets the urges of Hindu chauvinism, both raptured by the promise of the digital – that the full spectrum of corporatist nationalist authoritarianism glimmers into view.

ॾ

No equivalent, wholesale rollout has yet been mandated in Britain. One might envisage that in a fully functional Orwellian dystopia, the data-state would both nudge and coerce behaviours; that it would ably surveil and appraise our route of entry into the country as much as our economic contribution, our productivity, and our social, cultural and political behaviours and beliefs, crediting or removing privileges and ranking citizenship accordingly. The disqualification from voting rights, the withdrawal of access to services and provisions – bank accounts, passports, driving lessons – of those who failed to measure up would perhaps follow.

Dystopic data-states organised around datafied citizen-subject taxonomies of course came into view momentarily with the fraught efforts to impose vaccine passports: the biometric ID in rebranded, biosecurity form. Suspended for the most part for now, cultural conditioning nevertheless has begun, and technical infrastructures developed, not to enable, to be sure, disciplinary action as drastic or as final as citizenship deprivation, but certainly to institute an inevitably race-classed system of internal bordering asserting the right to exclude from aspects of social, economic, political and civic life all those without suitable data metrics.

Yet capricious efforts to introduce the vaccine passport were hardly the rebirth of a biometric identity database that originally died with the demise of Tony Blair, viscerally destroyed by Cameron-Clegg and celebrated as one of the major victories over the Blairite project. State-managed digital ID has been in progress for some time prior to the pandemic and continues to function in the background – the gov.uk Verify programme being its principal manifestation. Employment BDS (Boycott, Divestment and Sanctions) checks, universal credit applications, and rural payments are among the nineteen government services currently connected to the e-platform for identity verification by one of five private providers: Barclays, Digidentity, Experian, Post Office, and Secure Identity. NHS Digital has thus far managed to create over 22 million IDs – thanks to pandemic-induced disaster capitalism – and now sinks its claws into the nervous system of the NHS. And beyond this, landlords and employers – already responsible for administering border checks – are being encouraged to feed into digitised identity systems, while an accreditation system by the British Standards Institute certifying private organisations for complying with set guidelines is piloted, in efforts to ensure consistency and promote data sharing. Just as the installation of CCTV cameras in the 1980s relied on privatisation to counteract contestation against the semblance of a totalitarian state, so Britain's national identity architecture is set to reflect later stages of neoliberal statecraft with, as James Meadway and others note, the 'growing fusion of the powers of state and capital' in ways that distract from the state presence as it is popularly understood. Still, the political in-fighting between the nationalists, the libertarians and the corporate capitalist vanguard have thus far prevented anything close to coherence in a state-run national identity system.

For the libertarian right, devoutly anti any such big-state intervention, the vaccine passport – much like the mandate for mask-wearing – is dismissed as at the faux twin poles of Nazism and Stalinism. Indeed, prior to his premiership, this same sentiment was echoed by Boris Johnson himself when he claimed he would rather eat his papers than reveal them when asked for his identity. The 'freedom' from borders they call for, though, remains bounded and exclusive. As Richard Seymour observes, the 'creative-destructive' joys of life that right libertarians appeal to 'is in fact a heavily policed, bordered and violent society in which a lucky *few* are protected and secured'. The push here is for something akin to the floating good life of the Seastead Institute where the false promise of universal capitalist abundance means caviar for the rich and crumbs for the poor. Reaction here is not against bordering and surveillance but against state bordering and surveillance, implying that biopolitical controls and identity checks are not so problematic when controlled by Google. Even the 'non-partisan' libertarian Big

Brother Watch has not maintained its campaign against biometric ID cards since it has been administered by an amalgam of digital tech start-ups, multinationals and privatised state entities.

But fundamentally, the bounded and exclusive idyll that libertarians seek is premised on the maintenance of race-class bordering, where the use of biometric identification for preserving the sanctity of the nation is fully embraced. So Steve Baker can wax lyrical about the encroachment of state authoritarianism in the form of a Covid pass but remain committed to the introduction of voter IDs to keep out fraudsters. Nigel Farage sees no contradiction between his anti-biosecurity protestations and his steadfast commitment to HIV tests for migrants.

In countering reactionary libertarianism with reactionary state-managed neoliberalism, the centrist Labour Party's boring default response has been for sensible authoritarianism via the roll out of vaccine passports to revive a productive labour force and economy. The Labour Party's response was consistent with centrist politics of New Labour and its policy think tank reincarnation. Tony Blair and his institute have been waving the Bretton Woods flag for Britain, supporting business and industry interests which either stand to profit directly from identity creation – namely the digital ID industry – or those industries that see digital passports as the gateway to the resumption of more growth/accumulation: travel, tourism and hospitality. Excited, perhaps, about the prospect of returning to one of his long championed programmes for infrastructural change and modernisation, for Mr Blair and his people digital identity offered a solution both to the pandemic and to post-Brexit Britain's dwindling economy. Not dismayed by the lack of take up, the Tony Blair Institute is advocating for digital ID for asylum seekers, with which they are likely to have more success.

☭

The left has insufficiently grappled with the authoritarianisms birthed out of the security state and their race-class stratifying effects, which inhibit any hope of realising radical class solidarities.

On the one hand, the race determinist position, though sensitive to the realities of border control and policing, tends to fossilise racialised precarity in histories of postcolonial migration without reckoning with the class fracturing that this legacy has birthed. This position assumes that large swathes of British ethnic minorities, particularly those with roots across Britain's former colonies, are now vulnerable to citizenship deprivation – exemplified by a *New Statesman* article predicting two in five ethnic minorities in England and Wales would be eligible. But such blanket implementation does not map on to the contemporary coordinates of race-making and management in which racialised policing systems must also navigate an established brown and black globalised middle class. It is difficult, for example, to imagine the citizenship revocation of the middle class Sunak-Patel BJP-supporting British Hindu diaspora or those Brits whose sense of imagined community extends to supporting the Israeli settler-colonial project.

On the flip side are the left nationalists ill attentive to the full wranglings of the security state. Earlier concessions to securitisation, particularly via the domestic face of the War on Terror, indulged racisms for the sake of some social-democratic wins, nationalist welfarism and superficial multiculturalism. When state recourse to securitisation pivoted in new directions in response to Covid, fronted this time through 'biosecuritisation', and forged against fractured reactionary political faultlines, it was much more difficult for the left to muster a resolute, clear progressive response. Certainly sections of the left pointed to the discriminatory effects an identity pass would have, the redundancy of such a pass after a relatively short time when vaccine effects had worn off and the social cost of maintaining them, the individualisation of a collective public healthcare problem, the potential for exacerbating social inequalities, the role of vaccine passports in sustaining toxic vaccine nationalisms, and the further expansion and normalisation of data surveillance. But this discussion has proceeded in isolation from the parallel biosecuritisation and dataveillance that subsumes immigration control, an institution of the security state which ought not to be othered as elsewhere, or cast distinctly as the space where surveillance and policing mechanisms are tested, but seen as central to an anti-authoritarian, liberatory internationalist politics – particularly if we are to move beyond the constraints of challenging the demise of 'citizenship'. For now, retorts against vaccine passports are seemingly limited by their own nationalist constraints.

Out of the wreckage of this class fracturing and a strengthened libertarian right, the recent failed efforts to impose stringent biopolitical borders, at least internally, have brought some respite. But we need only wonder what the next political crisis will be, or when the next pandemic will erupt, to provide the necessary shock-enabling adjustment for the furtherance of mass data surveillance, for the systems and structures already in place to be made effective.

It is here in the chaos where hope for liberatory prospects lie, where an alternative might be salvaged.

GRACIE MAE BRADLEY

Peacetime

Words from the screen glow.

Any indiscriminate attack, especially one with impacts beyond the zone of hostilities, is a war crime. Otherside perpetrators will feel the force of our Alliance.

Dorothea half-opened her eyes into the harsh monochrome light. Headlines flashed down the wire by the Otherside onto newsprint for the coming day's stands.

OTHERSIDE GENERALS FLIP THE SWITCH

NO REST FOR THE WICKED

CHICKENS HOME TO ROOST FOR THE DEATH-MAKERS

Fully awake, Dorothea might have scowled as the First Minister spoke. But war and lone motherhood were exhausting and there were dreams to come.

G.

She watered the wilting dracaena and put it in the weak autumn light. She washed the mugs and took down the manager's sign threatening a broken-windows approach to abandoned teaspoons. No need to behave like the state over crockery.

Dorothea cleaned wax from rollers, refilled varnish jars, changed the acid bath, removed white spirits from the vicinity of every heat source. She had to sit at last at her desk in the light of the low sun. This had been her routine every day since being furloughed (how do you market plant-based supplements on the verge of total war?). Every day since V had left. Drop M off at nursery, sort out the studio, squeeze in an hour's work perhaps, collect her daughter again. Dorothea wondered whether they had any sugar soap.

She stood and the green vinyl floor squeaked and she caught her reflection in the window. Ten by eight panes per block, ten window blocks running the length of the studio. Eight hundred panes. The joy of art deco.

Thea you are not here to clean. Do your editioning.

I will.

She did not.

Dorothea picked up a copper plate and held it to the light.

She mostly worked from photographs, tracing them onto transparent paper, going over their lines with a needle on the waxed plate. This one had already been in the acid and the lines were etched deep. The cross of a small chapel, Sweetwater. The last holiday before M, and the war.

Now that southern coastline was ashes, thermobaric blasted wasteland where the goats and ridges used to overlook the sea.

Thea it is bad enough that you have not declared these last plates. You know they are desperate for copper. Finish them or donate them. Or go home.

Some of her friends had been making little algorithm-friendly runs. *Sous les pavés* and all that. None of their husbands had been conscripted. She couldn't stomach the kitsch.

She sat in the warm rust of the setting sun and her hand made shadows on the wall. What was her daughter doing? They let them nap on the floor in litters at the nursery. Dorothea was one of five and guilty that M didn't have a sibling to roughhouse with, especially after what had happened.

V might not come home.

The extraction fans had stilled. Dorothea realised she was shielding her eyes from a low beam. She wrapped the plate in tissue and stowed it gently.

G.

She put it away again the next day. No need for a pristine run of prints of a place that no longer existed. The master printmaker nodded good morning on his way to the acid room and Dorothea covered her face with her hands and let the memory of biting saline Sweetwater mornings well up, the scent of thyme and honey.

Dorothea took two small steel rectangles from her drawer and a photograph of what she and V called Big Bay, two trains' distance from their home. A sandy concavity flanked by marshland and pine forest, the sea to the east; bisected at low tide by a small burn. When that flow reached thigh depth, on cold days when wet feet were a danger, you could still slip across by the delicate metal bridge in the centre of the bay, narrow enough that you could run your fingers on the railings on both sides. At high tide, three concrete steps at each end would disappear to leave the pale blue frame ascending and descending into the same expanse, implacable, whispering *too late.* They had ignored the sirens the first time, taking their shoes off to reach the sky-bridge steps, and, if they hadn't run when they realised the waves were rolling in, they would have drowned.

She traced the outline of the bridge onto paper, marked the level of the sea. She turned to the plates.

file the edges to a bevel
sand the faces
white spirits, degreaser
hot plate
warm not hot for soft ground
hot not warm for hard
drag the wax, roll

gold up to the light
gloves, smoke, tapers out

M had welcomed the day disconsolate, wail after wail into the dawn light. The workshop manager looked at Dorothea as he affixed a new laminated sign about teaspoons above the sink. The dracaena wilted. Somebody turned on the radio and the First Minister extolled the virtues of rationing – 'think about it like a compulsory 5/2 diet!' For the first time in a long time Dorothea worked in the space between meditation and muscle memory. When the plates had cooled she inverted the tracing paper and marked the edge of the sea level on each plate. Onto one she scribed the outline of the sky-bridge, careful to keep the edge of her hand off the surface. Onto the other she pressed a single unbroken line in pencil to mark where sea met sky.

In the acid room she painted directly onto the plate with a small brush dipped in the corrosive, spit-biting out the detail of the cloud and waves.

straw hat the back stop out the edges
dry
acid bath 12 minutes

meths wax off
dry
mask aquatint drum
dust settled
flame

With a thick brush she covered the background of the sky-bridge plate with stop out varnish. She let it etch another two minutes in the acid, rinsed and dried, stopped out the bridge so that only the concrete steps remained, etched again. The most acid-eaten parts would hold the most ink and be boldest. She considered the second plate, deliberating on whether sea should be darker or sky.

She stopped out the area above the dividing line, etched again.

Dorothea only had an hour before she had to collect M. She frowned. She didn't want to work with the honest muted greys and indigos of a typical day at Big Bay. She wanted the print to look how she'd felt the last time she and V were there; psychedelic, incandescent. Salty and noisy. The sky-bridge she made aquamarine. She inked the sea burnt orange with red and brown lowlights, the sky and sky-bridge steps warm gold.

She slipped damp paper out from the blotters and laid it over the background plate on the press.

registration sheet

plate

paper tissue lambswool

crush

She repeated the process with the second plate, imprinting the sky-bridge over the sea and the sky.

After a day working in the inverse, Dorothea felt something uncoil in her as she studied the finished print. She saw blemishes on the background plate - she should have stopped them out - and a heavy hand on the ocean, which looked apocalyptic, aflame. There'd be time to try different colours tomorrow.

ᖚ

At the nursery door, Dorothea called out, 'Hello baby!'

'Ants, Mama', M shouted. 'Ants!'

The nursery workers gave Dorothea an update. A cheese toastie for lunch, four soiled nappies, poked another child in the eye possibly on purpose, a restless half hour nap, lots of talking about ants.

Evenings went quickly, at least.

'Ants in Grandma's garden, Mama. I squash one two three! Put them in juice. Emma there too.'

'When did you see the ants sweetheart? We haven't been to Grandma's for a while, that's why we said hello on the video at the weekend.'

'Today. Sleeping. Squishy!'

'Who's Emma, baby? A nursery friend?'

'With the ants. She's small. Hungry.'

Dorothea started to speak, was silent for a long moment.

'Well what a busy day you've had', she said at last. 'Let's moisturise your hair and then it's time to go buh-bye.'

Emma – that she had settled on that name.

For about two weeks, when she was three years old, Dorothea's mother had told her, she would go downstairs in the middle of the night and sit at the kitchen table 'making tickets'. After nights of putting her back to bed, her mother asked who the tickets were for.

All these people, Dorothea had replied, gesturing around them in the dark. *They're just passing through*!

When M was asleep, Dorothea started her own bedtime routine. A glass of whisky, a silk scarf round her hair. She turned on the news, which she ignored until nightfall. She lay down on the sofa, listened to the grey-eyed presenter's drone.

The Otherside this morning responded to fresh Alliance raids by announcing the deployment of an unspecified weapon on what they call 'a scale never seen before in history'. No impact on Alliance forces or civilian populations has been detected. After almost six months of fighting, and the capture of the Otherside's nuclear arsenal, the Alliance is close to achieving its war aims. Today's announcement has been called the enemy's last-ditch bluff.

Three soaking kittens approached Dorothea.

The scuffed laminate floor was a seething carpet of insects and pink-brown gelatinous invertebrates, and the room smelled of damp earth and engine oil.

Dorothea watched the kittens approach.

The writhing floor gave her vertigo and she tuned it out but she couldn't do so with the cats. They came on with the staccato movements of newborns, palm-sized tortoiseshell tabbies, mewling and keening. They were bedraggled and shivering, slick with oil or water. Their keens were insistent and outraged.

M's cries shot through the quiet house. For an instant they made an uncanny perfect fourth in the kittens' chorus.

Dorothea woke gasping. She rolled off the sofa, her breath heaving. She stumbled up and the child's screams continued. She ran to comfort her daughter, twisted in her sheets.

'Emma, no! Hurts!'

Dorothea held M, rocked her, woke her with gentle repetition.

'Sweetie, wake up, wake up baby, it's not real, you're sleeping, come on sweetie, it's OK, you're OK.'

M slowly opened her dark eyes. Her cheeks flushed deep brown, her curls were turned to frizz where she had pulled them out from under her bonnet in her sleep. She began to mumble. Dorothea's mobile sounded.

She swept M up into her arms and ran to it.

'V! V...'

'Thea sweetheart I have two minutes', her husband whispered over her voice. 'Two. Listen. We're shipping out again. I don't know what's making it onto the news over there but our guys are losing their minds. It's bad. You need to go to your parents.'

'V, what? Even the underground news says it's going well for our side, I thought we were almost ...'

'Thea I'm serious, go. And when you get there make sure the farmhouse looks abandoned. You need to stay awake and away from people.'

'What?' she said.

'Don't', he said. He sounded very far away. 'Please don't, please just do as I say.' She heard him breathe a long moment and she would have spoken again but he continued in a rush.

He said, 'I was on night watch last night and half of the guys fucking shot each other. They were barely even awake and they... Half the rest woke up and they shot themselves.'

'V *what*?'

'They were unravelling. Chattering about dead things.'

'Dead things?' That was her voice.

'Dead things', he said. 'Kills.'

'Kills? What?'

He tried to speak, his breath caught, she made it out through the static. He tried again.

'Every Otherside teenager hit by our attack on their convoy last week. Kills. Everyone who went down after we cut the lifeboat lines. Everything we've wiped out, ever, in our dreams. Every time. I can't –'

'What?' she said. 'V, what do you... I can't, V... Kills?'

He did not speak.

'Kills', she said again at last. 'Dead things. M...V, she won't stop talking about a girl, and about ants. And I saw...'

'Thea I don't have time.'

'Wait', Dorothea said. 'Emma.' She shifted M on her hip. 'She's...' She heard herself exhale, and speak again. 'M's talking about *Emma?*'

She heard him try to speak. 'Oh god. Thea I've been keeping myself awake for almost forty-eight hours and I can't, I...'

Another silence.

'This ... thing ... is radiating outwards. You need to stay awake. You need get out of the city. Please. Thea I have to go.'

Two breaths held.

She said, 'I love you.'

Dorothea listened to dead air. She put the phone down on the table next to where the kittens had been.

☭

The light was heavy pewter. Dorothea hauled out her cargo bike. She held her body against the front door to stop it slamming. M was swaddled in her snowsuit in the rear carriage. But for the afterglow of sleep, and the generous dose of medicine Dorothea had given her, she would have been protesting at the disruption to her day. They could not trust the roads. Too many people were desperate for fuel for her to be confident that there would not be trouble. A low moan emanated from a bedroom across the road.

Dorothea had weighed leaving at dusk. It would have given her more time to pack and board the windows. She would have showered the houseplants in the bath and put them in the most sheltered corner of the garden. She would have boxed up her notebooks with a handful of prized negatives, the photo album she called 'Old Friends Being Dumb As Hell'. E and M's first scans from when they were both still alive in her belly. Dorothea would have packed something that still smelled like V. She would have torn round to the print studio and emptied the first of each of her editions from the archive drawer, or her plates. But V had only had two minutes, so she and M had none, and she had wrapped her hair up tightly against the wind and cycled into the heavy morning, without an archive. M nestled among her meds, and some bottled water and turning fruit, and iodine tablets from the stockpile V had teased her about until things went so far that he had stopped.

She turned left into the park, sped onto the cycle path parallel to the river. It would broaden at the old flint chapel into a bridle path, and at last, after several cross-country miles, would reach her mother's farm. Dorothea turned up the volume on the little radio in her pocket so it spoke more loudly into her ear. Another emergency broadcast from a hoarse and even more clipped than usual FM.

Give me strength.

The first shots of true morning broke.

☭

The First Minister was a multiply decorated woman. She'd grown up in the same city as Dorothea. She had been an eloquent student radical. Not many people remembered that. Now she was festooned with medals, a veteran of three peacekeeping operations, two Special Ops drone extractions, and various 'presences' in the global South. The usual lot had complained. 'The Shoreditch Serial Killer', one placard called her. But her media nickname was BGB, the boss of girl-bosses.

Have you been fantasising about women ruling the world? a columnist had written when she won the election. *Me too!* Glass ceilings, final frontiers; layers of metaphorical barriers shattered, cracked and gave. Her social team clinched it. Geopolitics, seven-step skincare, and matronly scolding. Bend over the state matriarch's knee.

The First Minister was a multiply decorated woman, and, a week on from the Otherside generals flipping the switch, she may have been a boss but she hadn't slept in four days, because when she did she was mobbed by the dead: babies, old people, young men with kind faces. Every kind of livestock, rare birds, a pod of dolphins. And two vast entities frothing with cold and cavernous anger. A glacier, an ocean.

The First Minister was a multiply decorated woman in charge of Alliance forces which, mad with sleeplessness and shame, were self-immolating, drowning, shooting, auto-fragging, and those who did not do such things to themselves did them to each other and to the civilians near them, and the civilians were doing them to each other too.

The First Minister, when she had not slept in five days, being the First Minister, still had all the nuclear codes, both Otherside and Alliance, and, being multiply decorated and a boss, one grey morning marched red-eyed and still blow-dried in six-inch red-soled heels and a pastel lilac suit into the bunker under the Ministry of Peace and Prosperity, and punched in said codes and a pleasingly even distribution of coordinates, drawing a firm and final and bright line under the war, under the kills, under the Otherside, under all of them.

ALVA GOTBY

The Labour of Lesbian Life: Wages Due Lesbians and the Politics of Refusal

'It is the existence of lesbianism that makes fucking visible as labor' write Wages Due Lesbians Toronto in their 1975 founding manifesto; 'Fucking is work'. This statement formed the basis of the writing and activism of the group. Part of the international Wages for Housework (WFH) campaign, Wages Due Lesbians (WDL) were a network of Marxist-feminist lesbian activists mainly based in Toronto and London. While there has been a renewed interest in the writings of writers associated with WFH, such as Silvia Federici, Selma James and Mariarosa Dalla Costa, the WDL archives remain unexplored as a source of queer Marxist theory.

Wages for Housework was founded on the conviction that women's reproductive labour, often invisible and unwaged, is work that enables capitalist societies to function. The feminised work of caring for others is essential for ensuring that people can return to work every day, and for the generational replacement of the working class. WFH sought means for resisting this work, and thus for challenging capitalism. WDL put this into practice by refusing the labour of catering to men's emotional and sexual needs, thus hoping to disrupt the smooth functioning of heterocapitalism. To refuse such labour, however, is not a merely negative withdrawal of one's efforts. Rather it entails other practices, which are both similar and distinct from those of heterosexual women. In the WDL writings, lesbianism emerges not as a fixed identity but as a particular practice – one that involves the efforts of living a life outside of the institutions of the capitalist organisation of the heterosexual family. WDL thus conceptualised lesbianism not as the end-goal of the feminist movement, but as a collective organisational form based on both refusal of reproductive work as we know it and the invention of new types of sociality and different forms of life.

☭

Heterosexuality is a work discipline

In their diagnosis of life under capitalism, WDL argue that heterosexual families are a primary site for the exploitation of unwaged labour – the primarily feminised work of attending to the needs of others. Women's work, they suggest, is not only that of cleaning and cooking – the work of maintaining the physical health and capacities of the body – but also the work of creating and maintaining forms of subjectivities and desires. Under institutionalised heterosexuality, certain forms of desire come to appear as natural needs. These needs are taken for granted as the universal requirements of a good life. Yet the satisfaction of such needs results in the continued exploitation of women's undervalued and invisible labour of attending to men's sexual, emotional, and physical wellbeing. WDL thus define heterosexuality, in *Lesbians Organise* (1977), as 'a way of extracting unpaid and low paid servitude from women'. However, women are not passive victims of such social formations, but are rather its active participants and primary work subjects. In heterosexual marriage, WDL Toronto write, 'the woman supports the man to work harder, to buy a bigger house, a car, etc., and to subjugate her needs to these needs, which are capital's'. Heterosexuality is an institutionalised lifestyle that requires not only the sexual desire for a different-sexed partner but the social desire for a particular kind of life, and all the material underpinnings of that life. This desire compels both men and women to perform certain types of labour. Capital's need for specific patterns of consumption becomes near-identical with the workers' own need for a liveable life, and thus they also come to desire their own subjugation to work. For WDL, capitalism is always heterocapitalism, where sexual desire and emotional need have become bound up with certain forms of labour and the material, legal, and social institutionalisation of the heterosexual couple and the nuclear family.

In her 1976 article, 'The autonomy of black lesbian women', Wilmette Brown, a member of WDL and co-founder of Black Women for Wages for Housework (BWfWfH), suggests that heterosexuality is a work discipline. It is thus not merely an individual expression of desire or a sexual orientation, but the social organisation of life and labour. It extracts a certain amount of labour, especially for those who have been tasked with ensuring the wellbeing of others within the heterosexual couple or family. This labour simultaneously produces and depends upon particular subjective forms. It is also invisible as labour – if it were not, it could not appear as a natural and therefore non-political condition. For WDL, and for WFH more generally, heterosexuality and its attendant gender positions have to appear as simply *being* but are, in fact, doing, a highly particular practice that comes to appear as a natural state. The highly codified and institutionalised work discipline of heterosexuality, therefore, seems to be a merely private, natural, and intimate state of being.

Because sexuality is seen as private, there is a reluctance to understand it as work. According to Silvia Federici's 'Sexual work and our struggle against it' (2017), sexuality is constructed as 'the last stronghold in the division between the public and the private, which hides the degree to which our alleged private life is controlled and planned according to the same criteria that regulate factory work'. A central project of the WDL writings is to undo the mystery and romanticism which surrounds sexuality, appearing as a site of freedom from the regimentation of the waged workplace. Ruth Hall, a member of WDL London, argued in 'Lesbianism and power' (1975) that it is a common misconception, even among contemporary feminists, that sexuality is not political. These feminists participate in the liberal myth that 'what you do in bed is your own business'. This also suggests that there is a separation in capitalist life between sexuality and all other spheres of life. Sexuality is split off from all other activity. This is simultaneously a gendered, spatial and temporal separation, in which work time is distinguished from the temporality of sexuality. While many people mainly work with people of the same gender as themselves, 'our "leisure" and sexual activity is organised on heterosexual lines'. According to WDL Toronto, this serves to isolate women from one another as well as from their sexual partners, by separating the forms of intimacy that are seen as appropriate in the different temporal and spatial spheres of work and leisure. The heterosexual organisation of leisure fragments capitalist social life, making the private sphere the exclusive zone of acceptable sexuality, while outlawing other forms of relationality. For WDL, then, sexuality is confined to the 'private' sphere of heterosexual coupledom, whereas women's friendship and intimacy is constructed as devoid of sexuality. (Hetero)sexual relations are made to compensate for the impoverished state of all other social relations, in which sensual pleasures are taboo.

This heterosexual sphere is not only that of the heterosexual couple itself, but importantly also that of their children – the people who must be socialised and disciplined into becoming future workers. The work of creating subjectivity and desire thus becomes the work of reproducing such subjective investments in one's children. 'Women's work' is to teach children to desire the same things as their parents had – the same work discipline and the same social position. Capitalism requires not only the reproduction of healthy individuals, but also society itself. As much as capitalism seems to rely on constant change in social relations, it also depends on a great degree of continuity, in which children become adults by acquiring the desires and social habits of their parents. The reproduction of heterosexuality is both the means and the desired outcome of this work. It will ensure that future workers continue to adhere to a familial model in which their physical and emotional wellbeing is not the responsibility of their employers or the state, but instead relegated to the private sphere of the family. This also means that families are likely to be conservative in the desires and subjectivities they reproduce. In *Policing the bedroom, and how to refuse it* (1991), written after the rise and consolidation of the Thatcherite regime, WDL London state that '[m]onetarism – government by market forces – needs moralism'. Rather than a free market and a deregulated family structure, therefore, neoliberalism continued to rely on state regulation and more traditional ideas of the role of the family as an institution of reproduction, not only of people but certain conservative values.

For WDL, it is important to note that this arrangement of intimate life is detrimental for everyone – heterosexual men and women, children, lesbian and gay people. Hall states that '[o]nly the revolution destroying all productive relationships will destroy the hell hole of our sexual relations, lesbian and heterosexual'. Heterosexual men benefit the most from heterocapitalist arrangements, as their sexual pleasure and their need for emotional and physical comfort is given disproportionate weight. Yet the institutionalisation of heterosexuality, and its connection to the work discipline that structures men's lives in the sphere of waged work, serves to limit the lives even of those whose needs are most fully met. Those needs themselves are an expression of a deeply restricted, fragmented and regimented form of life. For those whose needs are not met by the institutionalised heterosexual family, life is precarious and fragile. They might achieve some freedom from the work discipline of heterosexuality, but all sexual and reproductive arrangements are restricted by the institutionalisation of the heterosexual family in the private sphere. As Beth Capper and Arlen Austin write in a 2018 essay for *GLQ: The Journal of Lesbian and Gay Studies*, 'BWfWfH and WDL impressed that "the home" disciplines the sexualities and labors of even those seemingly excluded from its domain'. WDL argue that it is necessary for both heterosexual feminists and lesbians to resist this arrangement, by various forms of refusal of heterosexual work discipline.

☭

Refusal and power

A core argument of the WDL texts is that lesbian relations are one way of resisting the capitalist organisation of reproductive labour. But this is not a complete refusal. They emphasise that one cannot simply opt out of capitalist society, and therefore every form of resistance and refusal will be partial. Lesbianism, as the Power of Women Collective write in 'At home in the hospital' (1975), does not free us from work. The lesbian separatist movement, they suggest, misdiagnosed the causes of women's oppression, by making men appear as the eternal enemies, thus missing the role of capitalist relations in institutionalising heterosexuality. It also, as WDL London note, locates the exploitation of women's labour solely within marriage. By contrast, WDL members argue that lesbians still participate in gendered reproductive labour in various ways – for other women, for their children, elderly people, in their communities, and at their waged workplaces. WDL offer a rebuttal of the critique often made of WFH – that the movement solely focused on married white women's labour within the domestic sphere. As Capper and Austin have argued, the writings of WDL and BWfWfH expand the field of housework by conceptualising it as something those excluded from normative domestic arrangements are still made to participate in. By refusing the heterosexual, institutionalised form of reproductive labour, WDL argue that lesbians are forced to reinvent reproductive labour in various ways. The refusal of work, as a political strategy, always carries an element of creative invention.

By including more forms of activity in the term 'work,' they also expanded the possibilities of political refusal. WDL writings apply labour tactics such as strikes, absenteeism, and wage struggles in our seemingly most intimate relations – those of the family. Love, they argue, is not a natural state in the relation between men and women. Rather it must be constantly produced. According to WDL, such production can be refused, a form of resistance that also exposes the power hierarchies that are part and parcel of the production of love and desire within heterosexual couples. Hall writes that lesbianism is a struggle against work 'in the obvious sense that relating to men is very hard work – sexual, emotional, and laundry'. Lesbianism emerges as a resistance to multiple types of labour, which form a continuum within heterosexual arrangement. WFH member Leopoldina Fortunati suggests, in *The Arcane of Reproduction: Housework, prostitution, labor and capital* (1975), that it is the emotional aspects of heterosexuality that make heterosexual women carry out housework such as cooking and cleaning for their partners. There are many reasons why women perform reproductive labour – not all of them are 'for love' – but love changes those work relations and makes it harder to resist the work discipline of heterosexuality. By rejecting this emotional and sexual aspect, WDL also reject the uneven distribution of unwaged care work and physical housework that characterise most heterosexual couples. In this way, WDL had a pivotal role in the WFH strategy as a whole, by refusing the most intimate and naturalised work of heterosexuality.

The WDL writings thus propose a politics based on a drastically rethought notion of sexual intimacy, both in suggesting that heterosexuality requires hard work and because it opens up the possibility for a different form of sexuality. This is inherent in their notion of refusal, which enables women to resist exploitative aspects of sexuality in order to move towards different practices. Francie Wyland, a member of WDL Toronto, writes in *Child custody, motherhood, lesbianism* (1976) that the practice of lesbianism undermines men's power to command sexual labour, not just for lesbians, but for heterosexual women too. This characterisation of sexuality also allows the category of lesbian to remain open, in that currently heterosexual women could move towards a refusal of their current sexual practices, thus creating the potential for something new. WDL member Ellen Woodsworth writes in 'Lesbians want wages for housework too' (1975): 'As a lesbian, I am refusing one area of the work that women are supposed to do – the sexual and emotional support of men. I know that by refusing that work, I am saying we can all refuse that work that society expects of us'.

An aim of the refusal of this work is to denaturalise heterosexuality – creating a practice that contradicted the seeming inevitability of heterosexual coupledom and family forms. Lesbian struggle, according to Hall, 'upsets the appearance that the capitalist organisation of our work is natural and inevitable and all for our own human needs'. Women's personalities and skills have been shaped to meet the needs of capital production and the men who are the main beneficiaries of the current organisation of reproductive labour. Both women's personalities as caregivers and the needs to which such caregiving responds are presented as naturally existing facts, rather than the outcomes of a certain organisation of production, inside and outside of the nuclear family. In their foundational manifesto, WDL Toronto state that the existence of lesbians shows that 'heterosexual love and marriage is not women's biological destiny'. Such denaturalisation is simultaneously a precondition and an outcome of lesbian refusal. The construction of lesbian sexuality as a form of struggle against the current organisation of work and society requires a view of sexuality as a type of reproductive labour, rather than a natural expression of sexual desires. Thus moving away from the naturalised nuclear family as the best way to respond to people's needs, WDL opens space for rethinking our sexual and emotional needs as part of the process of feminist struggle. As WDL London put it in *Policing the bedroom*, '[t]his rejection may not bring utopia, but it does help shake up all robotic intellectual, physical and social responses to the assumptions we have been force-fed'.

The refusal of the work of the heterosexual couple and family also created potentials for resisting other kinds of work. For WDL, lesbianism exists within a continuum of struggles against the exploitation of women's labour. According to WDL Toronto members, it is one form of refusal among many, opening the potential for a general disruption of the capitalist model of reproduction, which depends on women's low waged or unwaged labour both within the home and outside it. While lesbians were thus integral to the WFH practice of refusal more broadly, they did not construe their own activism or sexual choices as the only or necessarily most radical form of feminist struggle. In their critique of lesbian separatism, WDL members often return to their conceptualisation of the lesbian struggle as a necessary but not sufficient aspect of the women's movement more broadly. Separatism serves to isolate lesbian women from heterosexual women, argue WDL Toronto in 'Lesbian testimony presented at the International Tribunal on Crimes Against Women' (1977), who might also be struggling against aspects of the heterosexual work discipline. Differently located women within the social totality have access to various forms of refusal, which might be distinct from the decision to live without a male partner. In a statement in support of the decriminalisation of sex work, WDL Toronto and London argue that not only are many lesbians themselves sex workers, but that sex workers more broadly act in continuum with the lesbian refusal to have sex with men for free within the context of a romantic relationship. In a similar vein, Brown stresses that Black women's childbearing and seemingly unruly sexual practices can be read as a refusal of the capitalist sexual discipline based on white, bourgeois domestic arrangements. WDL thus construe lesbian refusals as part of a broader struggle against the sexual labour imposed by capitalism. As Capper and Austin write,

> [r]ather than assert strict divisions between 'straight' and 'queer' women, WDL framed heterosexuality in a manner far closer to Cathy J. Cohen's (1997) use of the concept of heteronormativity to describe how normative heterosexuality's state-sanctioned and institutional organization regulates and immiserates a range of social subjects (including those who may nevertheless engage in hetero-sex).

Hall also gestures towards labour struggles within waged workplaces in, for example, nursing, as part of the same denaturalisation process that lesbians engage in when refusing the labour of love within the heterosexual family. Women's reproductive labour, and their refusal of such labour, thus takes place within a dispersed network of sites and forms of subjectivity, and cannot be reduced to one form of refusal. The struggle against reproductive work could only be effective when starting from the perspective of a social total-ity in which differently located subjects' labours are intertwined.

This struggle was based on an organisational model in which differently located women formed autonomous yet interlinked groups. While WDL and BWfWfH were the most visible of the autonomous groups within the WFH network, the English Col-lective of Prostitutes and WinVisible, an organisation consisting of disabled women, were also affiliated with WFH. The purpose of these groups within the broader WFH movement was, as WDL Toronto explained, to make sure that the interests of these groups were at the forefront of the movement, and to build the power of the most marginalised people. This form of organising enables lesbian women to struggle together with heterosexual women without either risking being further marginalised or presenting their own struggle as unique or vanguard in relation to the feminist movement more broadly. According to WDL, organisational auton-omy permitted more oppressed groups to work together with less marginalised groups, on terms set by those with less power. Such a model was designed to foster a sense of solidarity, where those more marginalised were given a central place in the broader move-ment. It was also a question of power – only by strengthening the position of those seemingly most powerless, WDL London wrote, could the working class as a whole become more powerful.

Conceptualising their own struggle in this way allows WDL Toronto to argue that lesbianism is not in itself a victory. Contrary to understandings of lesbianism as itself an ideal form of sexual-ity, WDL insist on seeing lesbianism as an ongoing practice. WDL texts construe lesbianism as we know it as severely limited by the broader reproductive arrangements of heterocapitalism. But this also means that lesbian sexuality is a process rather than a finished identity. Lesbian struggle is a self-abolishing movement, which strives to undo lesbianism as a separate identity. Because lesbian identity is not external to the capitalist organisation of sexuality more broadly, it cannot be a solution to the patriarchal organisation of reproduction. Rather, it is an immanent potential for struggle.

For WDL, this struggle took the form of the demand for a wage. As WDL Toronto succinctly put it: 'For us lesbian women, wages for housework means wages against heterosexuality'. A wage for past and current housework would enable lesbian women to leave heterosexual households, giving them the financial independence needed to live without men. Against those critics who suggested that the WFH strategy would institutionalise women in the (heterosexual) domestic sphere, WDL Toronto members argue that more money would in fact give women more freedom to leave it. Being compensated for all the work women do, they insisted, would strengthen women's position and enable them to refuse that work. For WDL, it is women's generally financially weak position and low wages, combined with little access to the means of subsistence independently of men, that makes it difficult for many women to come out as lesbians. In the words of WDL London: 'We want the particular physical and emotional housework of surviving as lesbian women in a hostile and prejudiced society, recognised as work and paid for, so women have the economic power to afford sexual choices and can come out in millions'. This perspective also implies an analysis in which many lesbian issues appear as a result of women's low-waged jobs, and the seemingly biological imperative to perform reproductive labour for men in exchange for economic security. The fact that many lesbians lost custody of their children when coming out was linked to their inability to independently support their children, Wyland explained, as well as judges labelling lesbians as 'unfit mothers'. WDL Toronto also emphasise that lack of suitable and affordable housing is a barrier for lesbians who want to leave unsatisfying and abusive marriages with men.

Throughout their writings, WDL highlight the economic and material conditions of lesbian lives. Lesbian and gay visibility, they argue, is not a goal in itself but could only be the consequence of the collective mobilisation of queers to gain power and the material resources needed to secure liveable queer lives. Against the individualising emphasis on 'coming out', WDL Toronto stress that visibility is not a question of individual will but of collective power. Through their analysis of sexuality and class, they make the link between sexual choices and economic power, arguing against those parts of the left that saw the gay and lesbian movement as a middle-class concern. But WDL London also take a stand against the parts of the movement that sought respectability and influence for its most privileged members, arguing that only a working-class movement can bring about real change, as more affluent gay men were likely to opt for shallow notions of sexual diversity and inclusion over a structural reconfiguration of sexuality and domesticity.

For WDL, the lesbian movement must thus be concerned with building women's access to resources – a move that allows them to meet (and reimagine) their needs independently of having to perform reproductive labour for men. Such resources consist not only of material objects but of social bonds. Lesbianism, while not a solution to the contradictions of reproductive labour under capitalism, serves to increase women's power. Hall writes that 'our ability to live without men, our ability to express ourselves and our feelings for each other are in turn a source of power, just as money, time, facilities, even laws that we win serve to increase our strength'. Lesbianism also creates the space to redefine and experiment with women's sexual needs. WDL Toronto argue that these needs, which have been constituted in order to bring pleasure to men, can be reconfigured in ways that increase the power of all women. Yet this could also produce a backlash, in which the increased power and visibility of lesbians leads to heightened levels of violence against those women who refuse the labour of heterosexuality. Lesbian visibility, then, even when resulting in more collective power, can also lead to various forms of violence and isolation, which in turn produce the distinct challenges of reproducing oneself and others as lesbian women.

The labour of lesbian life

Lesbians, WDL argue, are faced with distinct forms of homophobic violence, perpetrated both by men and heterosexual women. Heterosexual men are likely to be the main perpetrators of physical violence against lesbians. Lesbians face various forms of punishment, explain Hall and WDL London, for stepping outside of the heterosexual work discipline, including sexual harassment. But more important, because more difficult to confront and address, are the various forms of structural violence that lesbians face in their daily lives. Here, WDL insist that heterosexual women, even feminists, often participate in upholding the heterosexual organisation of the home and the workplace. According to Hall, the relation between heterosexual women and lesbians is a power relation between 'those who are living according to the rules, who are accepted and established, against those who are abnormal'. In this relation, straight women act like 'agents of the state' – enforcers of an established work standard. Lesbians are branded as 'shirkers' for refusing the labour of heterosexuality, and thus stepping outside of women's established (heterosexual) experience of exploitation. Such refusals, WDL member Ellen Woodsworth explains, lead to the exclusion of lesbians from the position of 'real women' – a position that is dependent on servicing men emotionally and sexually.

It also leads to the persistent isolation of lesbian women, which Hall argues is one of the worst effects of homophobia on the daily lives of lesbians. Such isolation excludes lesbians from even supposedly feminist milieus created by straight women. Lesbians are excluded from the solidarity and comfort that comes from complaining about husbands and boyfriends together. Here, Hall's description is similar to Tamsin Wilton's characterisation, in 'Sisterhood in the service of patriarchy: Heterosexual women's friendships and male power' (1992), of heterosexual women's friendships, which function analogously to a battlefield hospital, 'to get the casualties fit and well so that they may be sent straight back to fight – not to rescue combatants from the horrors of war or to protest at war itself'. Heterosexual women's intimacy, including the feminist variety, might thus serve to uphold heterosexuality by tending to the emotional damage without questioning the source of that damage. In the same process, lesbians are excluded from the community of women and definition of womanhood, which becomes construed as the willing participation in one's own subordination. But, as Hall writes in 'Lesbian testimony presented at the International Tribunal on Crimes Against Women' (1977), 'the source of this crime is not women, but those in whose interest it is to keep women disciplined by heterosexuality'. One of the goals of autonomous lesbian organising, then, is to create autonomous lesbian power that would force heterosexual women to take lesbian practices and organising seriously, and foster solidarity among women of different sexual identifications. This also means not drawing strict lines between those identifications and thinking of them as stable and inherent, but rather conceptualising them as open to change.

According to WDL, the lack of visibility of lesbian women might serve to isolate lesbian women from each other. Women's limited economic independence, made more precarious in situations where discrimination against lesbians might lead to the loss of jobs and housing, also made it more difficult to create lesbian communities. For WDL London, this is expressed in the lack of specifically lesbian spaces. With their limited economic means, women have little capacity to create financially viable community spaces, especially in cities such as London where rent is high. But lesbians often find themselves moving from towns and rural areas to larger cities, WDL London write, in order to find what little community there is in the cities. According to WDL, then, the lack of material resources, and its attendant lack of visibility for lesbians, means that lesbians struggle to create and sustain communities outside of the nuclear family form. The institutionalisation of heterosexuality, including through various economic means, leads to a lack of sustainable alternative modes of sociality from which lesbian communities can grow. Queer experiments in community-building are often short-lived. This lack of resources to build community should also be understood as a more subtle form of violence against lesbians and other queer people, who might suffer physically and emotionally from the lack of available spaces and socialities to sustain them.

In such a climate of isolation, mental illness among queer people is likely to be frequent. Hall writes that '[i]n places where no other lesbians are visible it is an isolation that is right next door to madness, and often delivers us into the hands of medical institutions'. Add to this the fact that lesbians have long been likely to be branded as mentally ill, whether they experience themselves as such or not. According to Woodsworth, lesbians are women who step out of line, perverted and unladylike women – like those unruly women who are called 'crazy', engage in sex work, or rely on benefits from the state instead of the economic security of the nuclear family. As Wyland stressed, lesbian women's loss of custody of their children also relies on the stigmatised position of 'bad mothers' who are seen as performing social reproduction incorrectly, thus threatening the well-being of their children. WDL London wrote that 'lesbian women's mothering is under constant suspicion and scrutiny' – something that became more apparent in the aftermath of Section 28, the clause of the 1988 Local Governments Act which branded homosexuality as 'a pretended family relationship'.

These forms of discrimination and prejudice against lesbians and their families and communities led to an increased need for what WDL refer to as 'emotional housework' – all the labour that goes into comforting and caring for those experiencing the emotional harm of living in a hostile society. Hall writes that 'there's so much pressure all the time on all of us that we are continually having to struggle to hold each other together and keep sane. We're all mothers, all the time mothering each other and trying to keep a grip on ourselves'. There are thus two aspects of the reproductive labour that lesbians perform. Firstly, lesbians are still understood as women (though perhaps not 'real women'), and therefore expected to perform certain forms of reproductive labour for men. As members of WDL Toronto put it, the power relation between men and women 'is so pervasive in our lives that even when we stop sleeping with individual men, we are still expected to be servants to men on the job, on the streets, in school, etc.'. The gendered division of labour is thus not only located within the heterosexual couple itself, but stretches outside of it and shapes society.

Secondly, lesbians have to perform the labour of caring for one another, often outside of established institutions such as marriage. Part of this work is making sure oneself and one's partner are able to return to work the next day – work that is similar to that of heterosexual couples, including cooking and cleaning as well as emotional support. As Capper and Austin note, this analysis presciently portrays lesbian relationships as reproductive, at a time when homosexuality was solely associated with non-reproduction. At a time when lesbian lives were understood as more decisively outside of capitalist normativity, WDL thus understood lesbian reproduction as containing elements of capitalist labour, and not fully distinct from heterosexual social reproduction. Unlike many other gay and lesbian movements at the time, WDL theorised a homosexuality which could be at least partly integrated into normative social reproduction.

However, WDL add that part of the reproductive labour that lesbians perform is unique to those who are marginalised in society. This involves the labour of trying to compensate for the emotional harm of homophobia and the additional labour required of those who are trying to survive without material and institutional support. But it might also entail the labour of building communities and struggles that challenge the status quo, creating forms of sociality that are not based on exploitation. Marginalised people are compelled to reproduce themselves for capital, but also for themselves – inventing social forms that become sources of comfort and joy. Often these acts of invention sit somewhere between work and play, pointing towards new structures of feeling and collective forms of care.

WDL experimented with celebrating the supposedly lacking and unnatural quality of lesbian reproductive labour. Embracing the label of lesbians as 'bad mothers', Wyland states that '[w]e are demanding the power to be with those children *in a way that is not work*' (emphasis in original). For WDL, not living up to the standards set by heterosexuality becomes a point of pride. This includes the refusal to raise a disciplined and heterosexual workforce. WDL strived for a different way of relating to children – one that could be more playful and undisciplined, orientated towards pleasure in the present, rather than aimed at producing a future-orientated subjectivity characterised by a desire for the discipline of work and family.

In the decades since these writings were produced, capitalist social and emotional relations have changed. The hegemony of the breadwinner family model has been replaced by a dual-earner model, and divorce has become more common. While women still struggle with financial insecurity to a higher degree than men, many women have been able to opt out of the heterosexual family form. The feminist and gay movements have successfully challenged some of the restrictive and oppressive practices that are associated with the nuclear family. But we are also living in a time of violent backlash against queer and trans people, as well as misogynist tendencies which re-emphasise women's role as reproductive workers first and foremost. The term 'lesbian' has become associated with transphobic versions of feminism, although a majority of the women participating in the TERF movement are straight. Wages Due Lesbians London changed its name to Queer Strike, and continues to operate as an explicitly trans-inclusive group of queer women. Perhaps the moment of organising strictly under the banner of lesbianism has been superseded, yet given the unruly and queer legacy of the lesbian movement, we should be wary of giving up the term lesbian to the TERFs. The refusal of heterocapitalist work, a key part of the WDL tradition, lives on in queer movements.

In 1986, WDL London made a list of the work that lesbians do. One item on this list is '[h]aving to invent lesbian lives'. WDL do not understand lesbianism as a finished identity but rather an ongoing project – continual acts of invention. As all our sexual identities and practices are hampered by capitalist work ethics, the work of lesbianism is also the labour of inventing new social and sexual practices. Here, there is a similarity to the notion of queerness as that which is outside of institutional support, and which is therefore different for the homonormative modes of life that have strived to include certain same-sex practices within the institutions of heterosexuality. While showing that lesbians are forced to accept certain normative forms of labour for their own survival, lesbian practice also entails resistance to those forms of labour. In a time when the mainstream lesbian and gay movement has become increasingly integration-ist, we might draw inspiration from this understanding of lesbian struggle – as a practice not outside the constraints of reproduction under capitalism, but also not fully subsumable into the institution-alised sociality of heterosexuality. What WDL proposed was not just a refusal of the heterosexual family but familial forms of labour *tout court*. The labour of queer life, then, would be the playful work of inventing new ways of survival and flourishing, on our own terms, outside the privatised care and love of the family. Such practices of invention, in which many queer people already engage, might gesture beyond the current constraints of heterocapitalism. They also open up queerness as a practice of experimentation rather than a fixed identity category. Those who currently understand themselves as heterosexual, and benefit from the material rewards of heterosexuality, may potentially betray their loyalty to the status quo and become part of the collective struggle against work and for new forms of sociality and desire.

In the WDL writings, lesbianism is a set of practices of refusal of work, as well as new forms of labour. Lesbian struggle is thus one that seeks to reimagine life in a way that is less constrained by the regimentation of sexuality and the demands of unwaged and waged work. In trying to live life outside of the institutions of heterocapitalism, collective queer struggle can create the power to unsettle the gendered division of labour as a whole. This would in turn undermine the capitalist organisation of needs and desires, and point to a more liveable future. In arguing that lesbian lives contain both labour and refusal, both violence and power, WDL constructed an understanding of queer life as anchored in mate-rial conditions that always contain their own immanent potential for resistance. WDL tried to constitute autonomous lesbian sub-jectivity that would challenge the heterosexual regimentation of reproductive labour and potentially enable all women to refuse the labour that had been forced on them by virtue of their gendered positionality. Such refusal brings the challenges and possibilities of imagining life anew – where new forms of sociality can create space for flourishing outside of the constraint, exploitation and violence of the heterosexual family.

JACKQUELINE FROST

The Third Event: Part 2 (extract)

For Miri Davidson

In the abolished century, Atlanteans stood still allowing the mosquitos to loot their blood, saying: 'there is no irreplaceable absence'. They are all out getting wetted by the weather, eaten by the insects, interpellated by the laws that orchestrate exceptions. Their bodies appear, through the diaphaneity of these processes, as would haptic replicas – edgeless and unrepresentable – like a swamp annexed by a sea. The floating life, with its limitropes and leitmotifs, ceaselessly habituates itself to coveting displacement, here understood as whatever elements symbolise the non-presence of tempests, foam and phantoms. When the Atlantean body is most wounded they call it the flood body. When it is most mutant: the petroleum body, or the carnival body, or the communion body. Since the arrival of the third event, despite being submitted to an alternative futurity by the most risky object of eras, Atlanteans will rescue the bee from the wave and struggle to involve themselves in its truth. Conversely, they dash cabbages, torn silk, rosaries and aspirin into circumoceanic currents in the deep-water convection. Potatoes, linen, hymnals, lecithin; collards, cotton, gris-gris, gelatin: all one in the end despite recompositions. 'Do not save love for things', they say, 'since outside the night is government'.

Here, the almost-earth is animated by a porous field of asphodels whose capricious mellifluidity, being neither sorry nor faithful, makes for an awkward augury. Meant to discover the structure of the third event and getting only so far as the temporal fabric, woven into an eschatological spectre, the archeologist, being tipsy, is ready to believe anything. 'The third event: wave and particle? Light-bearing ether or liquefied gas?' The purpose of this reconnaissance involved sketching an archeology of the future catastrophe using a method derived from the peripheral freedom of minor science. The assemblage of atlanticity, in its capacity as meta-narrative of mercurial objectivity, was conceived to address the cruel coordinate in the hardcore conduit, where we find the dead on the lips of the living and the living on the lips of the specialists. Taking a pirogue into the flotant, the archeologist examines watermarks left by the deep-water horizon. From them, she diagnoses the restoration of the flood's authority as an epiphenomenon of surplus heat involved in the fabrication of all this cheap alchemy. Just as before, the cane was a sweet machine of fealty extraction. Reconciled to field clothes that reek of bagasse and to stumbling from the rum, each day the archeologist watches the refineries burning the largesse.

It is for the sake of a militant fraternity that one passes through a dead culture in the ethnographic present, trying to make for oneself a community of inexistent others? Being a visitor to this continent's infamy, the archeologist observes that her hosts are plagued by the imagescape of their belonging to nothing but the ruin of the ruin – the inner, endogenous ruin that resides in the supersensual aspect of the ruin's archetypal instantiation. According to the civilisational categories of the archeologist, the only elements within the deep ruin that remain recognisable despite decomposition appear to be the steps of a stadium, the floors of a prison, the baths of a governor. Indifferent to criticism by non-Atlantean experts who claim that current policy engenders traumatic repetition, the city proposes that these catastrophic anteriorities, which embody the very destruction of Atlantis, serve the population as shelter during future storms, actively blockading other havens. Those that choose to not choose between the sensation of drowning on dry land and the sensation of drowning in water are said, by Atlanteans in hushed voices, to be working inside the third event. The Bureau of Land Interpretation calls these, in an improbable triumph of bureaucratic wit, 'the saps'.

Out in the world, empathic limitation structures the heart, the way sound and shadow structure eternality, the way color structures attention and accident. Is adaptation a value for those who happen to possess it? For whom is the deep a house? The third event, tropicalist and prehistorical, dwells in the *voilerie* – mending veils by day, tearing veils by night – eager to portend through overangelness a way out of this disaster ambiance. The nearest utopia is overgrown with bromeliads and a metaphysics of opaque essences. From its highest point, one can watch principalities conspiratorially flooded and sunk. Terrorised by the gaudy insurances of the elite, those born in the common colony use the past as a serum to treat – often unsuccessfully – transcendental sicknesses. Using the jingle, 'but is modernity's pursuit properly sensuous?', the past was peddled in snake-milk to the populace. Altanteans, reflecting later on this period, have said, 'We felt the great past might mend a little if we bowed low enough, if we succumbed and gave homage'. But the non-Atlantean dead, too, have committed some prolix portion of the evil of this night, owing no less to their notoriously toothless intercontinentalism. Naively, these claimed that if the Atlanteans wish for theirs to no longer be a secret out of the past, they should simply resurrect it, with a few ethnic songs and dances or little spell sacks of pepper and moss. Made of exterior calm despite the misery of planets, the third event practices the circumvention of elegiac existence, anticipating the arrival of a placeless energy.

For now, the chicanery of rulers is a practice of ambiguation realised in burnings and revivals. Proclaiming that the pure crest of the idea ruins everything, they begin their séances by writing in the book of machinations that all shall be subdued in the common sorrow. They are involved in the integrity of farcical deadening and the ritual transformation of feeding blooms with rust. They commence to moaning in strange liquid tones, intoning that the territory of the sea, their domain, is set to increasing. They agree that the beliefs of the mass are like weather, but forced through uncertainly, such that their dispossession must become arrow-like. They make sacrifice to the serial opacity of the hardcore conduit, regaling in the people's unbearable silence and fascination, held dihedral through throng and technique and private scandal. Their sessions invoke 'Our lady of the wrought iron cemetery ornaments; Our lady of the un-liberated capitals of suspect progress; Our lady of the no-less-ridiculous sexual arithmetic; Our lady of the hegemony of the limited fantasies of skin; Our lady of the teeth of the night in the mouths of the fisherman; Our lady of the incomplete spirits of martial law deployments; Our lady of the illegitimacy of non-market mediation; Our lady of the little wars and little military exercises; Our lady of the righteousness of corruptible love; Our lady of the zombified genealogy of guerilla science; Our lady of the tomorrows that sing in sub-atomic keys; Our lady of the relentless whiteness of doom's music; Our lady of the dull machetes of the deltaic populations; Our lady of the bad factories of indisputable goodness; Our lady of the revolt as a clumsy thief in the night'. They permit the ascension of a few chosen peasants, full of deeds but not thoughts, picked from among those who put small strokes of blood on the okra, committing themselves to the enormous bliss of Atlantean death. They despise the scythers, who receive the children of the workers blue in the gaslight. They have observed beggars full in their midsts, wondering why these do not take them by the throat or set fire to their houses, but wander instead through burnt cane muttering, 'there ought to be magnolias somewhere in this dusk'.

Paouelle says she has prophesied their meeting by 'the water of these desires'. The fieldwork is the museum of their encounter. The archeologist begins her interview asking, 'Do you saps believe in a deep form of life? Do eternal things endure it?' According to Paouelle, the night is not premeditated, though its been going

unconscious problem of being born in the common colony, submitted to the desolate miracle of all the devils and all the saints, to the sexuality of the garden, and to the ovaries of the female sago palm, to the social uplift of the night, to the ethos of the ethnos who is one blood cut up in lengths, to the orchid moth whose name in Atlantean means, 'memory of the future', to the moth orchid whose name means 'prophecy of the past', and finally to the desperate medicinality of music to which the Atlanteans often incant the saying, 'You've got to believe in the sound. It's the one good thing that we've got'.

It is recourse to prayer and not to historicity that is disseminated as plot to salvage the floating wreck of fabled destruction. What in other geographies in recent times might be called 'the intellectual' cannot be reconciled by ethnographic translation, since the project of the humanisation of Atlantean humanity, being uncreated, gleams oxymoronic. Rather, the word is idiomatic for a certain fragility that one associates with wounds that though scarred continue to reopen in the opposite shape of duty. This condition was, as it occurred among the commoners, non-contagious. Like any other figure of excess seeking revelation in a world indifferent to questions and answers, to be intellectual in Atlantis would involve negotiating the general perception of one's person as dragging around a body full of sybaritically perforated blood. Otherwise, the word for intellectual is used, though rarely, to describe thunder coming down in an unjustifiable meadow where neither land nor water insists. Any love for the ideas of things is said to dis-encounter the problem of justice, rejecting the laborious melancholy of a non-collective rearticulation of bones and needs. Individuality is assimilated to infrastructure or to a secret paranormality of the curse tropic. Its traces, however, seem to secrete themselves as from sleep, taking on the patina of a meta-theoretical element in the total climate.

TONY WOOD

The Invasion of Ukraine One Year On: An Interview

This conversation took place in February 2023.

Salvage: Is Putin likely to lose this war? Until recently it seemed inconceivable. Now there have been a series of tactical routs by Ukrainian forces, and Russia's 'partial mobilisation' has apparently engendered some cracks in Putin's domestic authority without necessarily adding much to Russia's military momentum. Is there a realistic chance now that, through military debacles or domestic breakdown, Russia loses?

Tony Wood: I would be wary of making predictions about battle-field outcomes – mainly because I'm no military expert, but also because there's just so much contingency in the day-to-day course of any war. That said, it seems to me that the overall set-up on both sides is more likely to produce a long stalemate than a clear victory for either side. It's certainly conceivable that Ukraine will make a breakthrough, forcing a full Russian retreat – conceivable, but unlikely. After Ukraine's impressive advances in the late summer and autumn, Russia dug in across the Donbas, and is clearly willing to throw massive amounts of men and *matériel* into holding something like the current front line. Russia's need – political and strategic – to avoid further retreats has often outweighed tactical considerations. This is also true of the war as a whole: Putin is committed to pursuing his objectives in Ukraine even at a tremendous cost to his own side. On the internal front, it seems to me that Putin is betting the war itself will stave off domestic breakdown rather than accelerate it. He may not be wrong in making that calculation, especially if the Kremlin succeeds in portraying this war of aggression as a defensive struggle against the West – a matter of 'national survival'. This would, of course, also make it harder for opponents of the war to gain traction.

Do the criticisms of Russia's military strategy by figures such as the Chechen leader Ramzan Kadyrov and Evgeny Prigozhin, a Putin confidant and owner of the mercenary Wagner Group, represent a serious fissure in the regime? Is the apparently disastrous miscalculation made last February having any consequence in terms of recomposition inside the ruling bloc?

On the question of fissures: no, I don't think so. There may be disagreements about the conduct of the war – there's nothing like battlefield failure to prompt finger-pointing – but in terms of the rationale for the invasion, the strategic view of Russia's place in the world, and its relation to its 'near abroad', the regime seems broadly unified. Prigozhin and Kadyrov are just jockeying for power and personal profit within a wide pro-war consensus. It's true that Putin doesn't seem to have prepared the country's political class as a whole for this war; apparently, he only discussed it with a very narrow group of advisors. But then, the fact that everyone fell into line so quickly suggests there was little interest within the elite in opposing it. Who knows, there may be figures within the regime who think the whole project is insane and are waiting for it to end in disaster so they can crawl out of the woodwork. But I don't think a palace coup is likely. These people know they will all go down together if Putin falls, so they are very unlikely to turn on him even if the war effort is going badly.

On recomposition within the ruling bloc: this remains to be seen, but my sense is that the war is deepening shifts that had already begun. Military spending has been on the up for several years, and the 'power ministries' – security services, military, intelligence – have always been prioritised under Putin. Meanwhile, the economically liberal wing of Putinism has been in retreat for at least a decade; and since 2014, economic policy has been geared to the wider imperative of withstanding Western sanctions. The war effort has accentuated all these features, though it's true that the allocation of much larger chunks of the state budget to military procurement is making the economic weight of the military much greater. But even there, the war will not necessarily bring a full return to a Soviet-style military-industrial complex or a planned economy. A significant amount of the fighting is being subcontracted to Prigozhin's private army, for example (which includes convicts recruited directly from Russia's prisons). So this war is a kind of public-private partnership, redirecting yet more state revenues into oligarchic hands.

In September 2022, at the time of the partial mobilisation, there were some outbursts of popular protest and apparently spontaneous resistance to recruiters, as well as flights to the border. Has there been any sign of a broader anti-war movement in Russia, or is this still muted?

Even before the war, there were very tight restrictions on public protest in Russia, making large-scale mobilisations risky and rare. Conditions have become even more draconian since then, and though there have certainly been outbursts of resistance, as you say, I haven't seen signs of an anti-war movement as such – that is, semi-coordinated groups of people publicly voicing the demand for a cessation of hostilities, at a minimum. This may yet emerge, of course. But the odds are stacked against it at the moment, given the repressive climate in Russia. There's also an issue of personnel: a lot of the people one could imagine helping to organise such a movement have had to flee the country. But it's also a wider political problem, and one those of us in the West who opposed the Iraq War should be all too familiar with: how to frame and organise mass opposition to an immoral war of aggression in conditions of generalised apathy or disengagement? And even if one succeeds, how to bring that political force to bear on the course of the conflict itself? We have to hope Russian opponents of the war can get somewhere with these problems, but it's a very tall order.

Has Russia applied the kind of kinetic force in Ukraine that it did in Syria or Chechnya? This sort of offensive was widely predicted by anguished pundits at the outset of the war, but – notwithstanding the severely brutal attacks on some cities such as Mariupol – this doesn't seem to have been borne out. Is that correct? And if Russia is being more restrained, why?

I wouldn't say there has been much restraint. Russia's large-scale attacks on Ukraine's electricity infrastructure just as winter was setting in would be one example of mass targeting of civilians, but there have been many others. Missile attacks on urban areas have wrought very serious damage and caused a lot of casualties. People in major cities are living in the basements of bombed-out buildings, just as they did in Chechnya. And the use of 'filtration camps' for civilians in occupied areas is very much comparable to Russian methods in Chechnya.

It is true that this war has not been fought from the air as much as many might have expected – at least, not by human pilots: both sides have made extensive use of drones. But it's also true that Russia's use of aerial power has been constrained by Ukraine's air defences. This is a major point of contrast with Syria and Chechnya – the Ukrainians have been able to fend off a lot more of Russia's ordnance. There may also be some strategic factors at work here.

For one thing, if Russia had used massive aerial bombardments from the outset, NATO might have found it harder to resist calls for a 'no-fly zone', which would, of course, immediately have brought a serious escalation. So it's possible Russia may have calibrated its approach in the early stages of the war to apply the maximum amount of force short of what NATO would consider grounds for immediate intervention. But secondly, and I think more importantly, once the initial Russian attempt to capture Kiev failed, the whole character of the war changed. In my understanding, the Russian army is much more geared to fighting this kind of long land war, and that's certainly what has taken shape in Ukraine.

Alexei Navalny, Russia's leading oppositionist, has been in jail since January 2021. How should we understand his position at the moment? He has been opportunistic, and engaged in anti-immigrant populism in the past. His politics would appear to be broadly centre-right. Yet his defiance from his prison cell appears genuinely courageous, especially as he's looking more emaciated. Does he have any realistic chance of leading an opposition movement? If so, how wary should we be of its politics?

Navalny is a paradoxical figure – both opportunistic and genuinely courageous, as you say. His politics have shifted a fair amount since he first came to prominence in the 2010s, from a broadly neoliberal stance framed in anti-corruption language – you could sum it up as: 'if it weren't for these crooks we'd have a thriving market-based system' – to something with a more social-welfarist emphasis. One place where this became especially visible was in the platform for his 2018 presidential run (blocked by the courts): for example he raised the problem of inequality and supported increased spending on healthcare, infrastructure, and social welfare. I think he realised around then that a neoliberal programme would not be that popular outside the major urban centres, and that to gain a truly national political reach he would have to propose some kind of social agenda. This is still true, and the consequences of the war are likely to make it all the more pressing. But I don't know that

Navalny has much chance of leading a movement from jail, and it would take some major shifts for the Kremlin to let him out. I think he was well aware of this, which is what made his decision to return to Russia in early 2021 so courageous. (He had been the victim of a near-fatal poisoning attempt the previous August and had to flee to Europe for treatment. But once he recovered, he returned to Russia, and was jailed on arrival.)

As for how wary we should be, the Russian left has certainly been split on this in the past – either oppose Navalny and risk irrelevance, or support him in the hopes of shaping his agenda, but risk being dragged along by a movement with goals inimical to the left's own. The war has rendered a lot of this moot, of course. But the fact that the Kremlin's most significant opponent has come out against it is important. Even if Navalny's anti-war stance is opportunistic – I can imagine a previous version of Navalny taking an equally opportunistic nationalist line, for example by supporting the war but criticising the way it's being conducted. And Navalny's backing would be a big plus for the Russian anti-war movement, if and when it emerges.

What should we hope for? The Western anti-war left has been split, not over whether to oppose Russian aggression, but over the degree to which we should support Ukraine (partly given Zelensky's internally repressive behaviour), over whether to support – or at least not oppose – arms from London and Washington, and over whether it would be better for Russia to be militarily defeated (which would give the hawks in those capitals a massive boost), or for a stalemate to result in ceasefire negotiations (which might reward Russia's actions with some territorial aggrandisements). Toward what outcome might our sympathies and efforts be best directed?

It seems to me there's a tremendous gap between what we might minimally hope for and what is at all likely to happen – all the most probable scenarios are bleak in their different ways. Viewed in broad geopolitical terms, I can imagine some on the left wishing for a stalemate, with both Moscow's and Washington's plans being blocked. But while that might well be what ends up happening, it's an unconscionable thing to wish for – it's a terrible outcome for Ukraine, condemning the country to serve as the battleground for rival imperialisms, the Flanders Fields of the twenty-first century.

In a basic human sense, we might wish for an immediate end to hostilities and a turn to negotiations. But politically, there are some serious problems with taking such a stance now. Earlier in the war the demand for a ceasefire and negotiations might have made sense, for example when Zelensky floated the idea of neutrality plus separate talks on the status of Crimea. But both Russia and Ukraine's Western allies rejected that, and since then the whole complexion of the war has shifted. Now it's not clear what the parties would even discuss, so the call for negotiations is at best an abstraction.

Russia's annexation of the four eastern provinces in September 2022 was a turning point: it massively raised the stakes and at the same time removed any incentive for the parties to negotiate. No sovereign Ukrainian government could accept the dismemberment of the country, while Russia's formal annexation of these territories – as opposed to occupying them for strategic leverage, say – made clear it was committed to doing precisely that. These are not negotiable positions, and something fundamental will have to change in order for either side to shift. In the short term, this could be a decisive defeat or victory for one side, in the medium to longer-term a serious challenge on the domestic front in Russia. But my fear is that we are in for a very long war of attrition, and that it will be a long time before anyone thinks of negotiations. We should, of course, continue to hope for them – but not expect them soon.

From where we now stand, it seems almost delusional to try imagining what a 'good' version of an eventual peace might be. But for the left, there are precedents we can draw on – ironically, in the very Leninist tradition of thinking about national self-determination whose legacy Putin is so determined to destroy. Recognition of Ukraine's sovereignty and right to democratic self-determination, allied to a rejection of what Lenin termed 'Great Russian chauvinism', would be the basic starting point. But it would be vital for the application of this principle to be accompanied by a process of democratic self-determination in Russia itself – unshackling popular sovereignty in order to curb Russian imperial ambitions. All of this runs directly counter to the current thinking of Russia's entire political class. So beyond hoping for their military failure in Ukraine, the left should hope for a broader transformation from within that dethrones their entire worldview. But again, this all seems very far-fetched from the standpoint of the present.

Following on from the previous question, would you agree that this situation gives an example of the limits of an – understandable! – internationalist left desire to 'call for' things, or 'oppose' things? Of course, we often rightly have to take positions we have little to no immediate chance of enacting and which outline a politics of radical solidarity: for example, in welcoming refugees from the – any – war. But there are concrete situations which will not resolve into any 'least bad' option for which we might 'call' in geopolitical and/or 'kinetic' terms. For example, if we allow that Ukraine has the right to resistance, it's hard to see the 'harm reduction' position many on the left have taken in firmly opposing any arms supplies to Ukraine as not amounting to a position that 'Ukraine has the right to resist, but the least-bad option will be if it loses quickly'. Conversely, to actively cheerlead arms-sales to Ukraine, let alone to 'demand' them, undoubtedly cleaves with the agenda of Euro-American imperialism. Can such circles be squared? In such a situation, the left can analyse and stand in solidarity, but, absent mass radical pressure, can we meaningfully 'demand' anything geopolitical or kinetic when the options and agents available to enact any such demands are inimical to freedom?

It's certainly true that the left's positions on this war are irrelevant to how it will unfold. Though I'm sure Ukrainians will welcome solidarity in all its forms, the question of whether the left opposes or supports a given course of action is mainly significant in terms of its internal repercussions. Which is not to say it's not important: there is a genuine need here to think through what principles are at stake, what the left values or wants to defend. I've mentioned the concept of self-determination, which is central to my thinking about this – I see it as the core of any tenable peace, but also as an inherent political good in itself.

Yet in the absence of mass radical pressure, it is also fraught with dangers, as the example of the former Yugoslavia shows. Many observers have noted that the war in Ukraine could be seen as a much-delayed war of Soviet succession, equivalent to the 1990s conflicts in the Balkans. This raises a larger analytical point that bodes ill for the post-Soviet space as a whole: in a longer-run per-spective, one might argue that the former Russian empire has yet to complete the whole process of nation-state formation that ravaged the rest of Europe for centuries. The Soviet model both arrested and assisted the development of many diverse nationalisms across the USSR's breadth; with that system's collapse, we have seen the development of new nation-states – now in neoliberal conditions, sundered from any idea of social transformation, as Volodymyr Ish-chenko and others have observed. What this means, I fear, is that the war in Ukraine may only be the prototype for a string of wars in which similar dilemmas will apply.

A major part of the problem here is that such wars will mostly be waged in terms alien to the left, pitting rival nationalisms and imperialisms against each other. In the case of Ukraine, its entirely legitimate struggle for national self-defence has become entangled with the US' project of global dominance, which the left naturally opposes, facing off against a Russian neo-imperial advance, which the left also opposes – hence the unsquarable circles you mention. But if the left was more powerful, the dilemmas might if anything be more severe. The example of the European Social-Democrats vot-ing for war credits in 1914 springs to mind – a salutary reminder of what can happen to even a large and organised mass move-ment in conditions of inter-imperial warfare. But perhaps there's also something useful to be gleaned from that historical moment, in terms of the need for the left to escape the geopolitical logic of inter-imperial contention – that is, to make its demands not within that framework, for or against a given position, but to transcend it, while still acting in solidarity with those most oppressed by it. I'm obviously not suggesting that we should just rehash the Bolsheviks' 'Peace, Land and Bread' agenda of 1917, or that we can magic up a new iteration of the Zimmerwald left's class-based, international-ist opposition to the First World War. But it's worth thinking about what would be the functional equivalents in our times of those radical acts of systemic reimagination.

RICHARD SEYMOUR

BIRDS

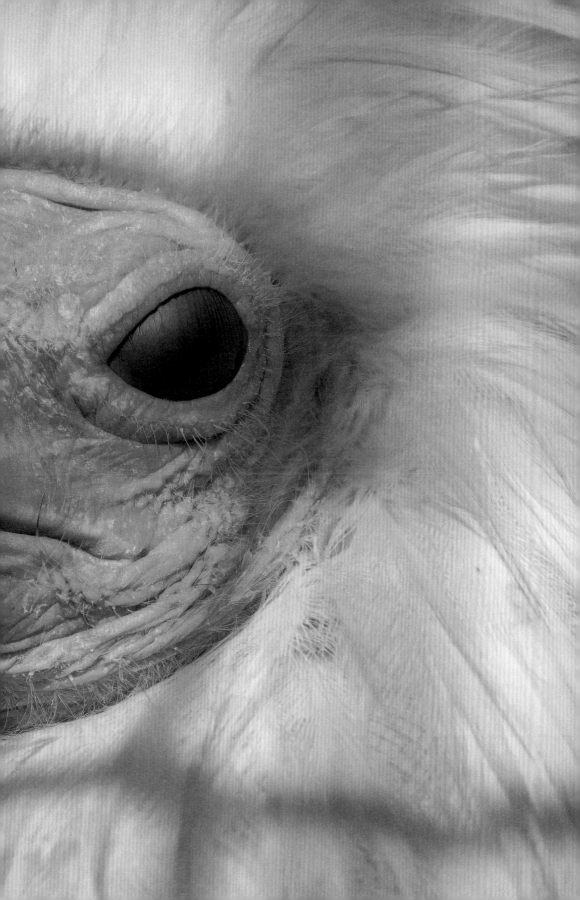

JAMES MEADWAY

Time, Labour-Discipline, and the End of Industrial Capitalism

It has been more than three years since the World Health Organisation reported the outbreak of a novel coronavirus in Hubei province, China, on 9 January 2020. Three months later, the WHO declared Covid-19 a 'public health emergency of international concern'. Six months after that, following a deliberate, global demobilisation of social and economic life unknown in human history, deaths from the SARS-CoV-2 virus passed the one million mark. Total infections from the virus today are estimated to be over 300 million; total deaths, 6.5 million.

Yet this initial, devastating shock is likely only to be the first impact of the virus itself. Contrary to the (absurd, in hindsight) prognoses that either the virus would 'pass over' the population quickly, or that vaccines would magically end the infection, the appearance of the Omicron variant at the end of 2021 and its rapid spread across the world was an indicator that the foreseeable future remains subject to severe dislocation. Eradication or even elimination look even more fantastical: with SAR-CoV-2 now present in animal populations close to humanity, and with 'reverse zoonosis' from such a population one of the probable sources of the Omicron variant – according to recent research reported in *Science* – management of the virus will impose significant costs from here on in. The costs of vaccination and revaccination, the costs of screening, the costs of health and care system capacity: these are substantial new burdens for the foreseeable future. Strange new side-effects are being revealed: a sharp rise in deaths from heart disease among those previously infected with covid, reported in *Nature*; the misery of 'long covid', and the costs of managing it; the resurgence in viruses thought somewhat tamed, like monkeypox and polio, with their own complex bio-social relationships back to Covid-19.

We will not be returning to the pre-pandemic world: not as lockdowns ease, not if vaccines are put into every arm, not ever. We should, if the epidemiologists are correct, get to a form of endemic Covid-19, with some luck and a successful global vaccine rollout, over coming years. But the path there will be uneven; as we are already seeing, not only are vaccines themselves unevenly distributed, the distribution of vaccines does not, by itself, remove us from the disease environment we have created for Covid-19. The virus marks the entrance of the global economy into a period, unknown for as long as a capitalist, global economy has existed, of stagnation and decay. It is the first clear marker of a future in which the foundational certainties of the past two hundred years of industrial capitalism, built on the twin principles of maximising exploitation of labour and extraction from nature, are thrown into doubt and, with them, the principle of near-assured and cumulative economic growth that underpins the stability of developed economies. It is, as economic historian Adam Tooze suggested in the early months of this pandemic, 'the first crisis of the Anthropocene'.

ᕤ

Understanding Covid-19 economics

Much of the (inevitably voluminous) writing on Covid-19 has failed to capture this novelty and severity. For economics, the most conservative of all the social sciences, the tendency to assume reversion to a steady mean of steady growth and that 'exogenous shocks' fade over time has led to a dramatic understatement of covid's long-term impact. The failure of economists to look more closely at the virology or the epidemiological modelling, pointing to a prolonged period of instability not easily compared to (say) pandemic influenza, has resulted in some absurdities: in Britain's official forecasts, not only is Covid-19 not as bad as Brexit in its long-run impacts on the British economy, but it is precisely half as bad as Brexit.

At the level of mainstream theory, meanwhile, attempts to model economic responses to Covid-19 on the basis of rational or near-rational individual 'utility maximisation' has produced bizarre results. Mainstream attempts to think through the consequences of covid have tended to underplay the shock it has presented to *institutions*, and so significantly understate its likely long-term consequences in favour of focusing on individual behaviours. Like economist Alwyn Young's modelling of the HIV epidemic in southern Africa, which confidently predicted a positive long-run growth impact from HIV because of its negative impact on fertility, the mainstream has zeroed in on the question of how rational consumers might shift their 'preferences'. The barrier to economic recovery, in this world, becomes 'fear' of the virus amongst consumers, rather than the virus itself or the response of the institutions that shape individual actions and possibilities. Conventional macroeconomics, even where more obviously influenced by Keynesian thinking, has tended to view the primary difficulty related to covid as its impact on consumer and business spending – and therefore to understate the risk of sustained inflation arising from supply-side impacts.

Yet even the more radical attempts to apprehend the pandemic through its 'biopolitical' impacts understate its novelty. For the anti-science conspiracy theorists – given a high theory gloss by a former star of the left academy, Giorgio Agamben – the impositions of lockdowns and coercive vaccination are nothing other than a monstrous assertion of pure biopolitical power against human life. The material reality of the virus – the fact it really will kill at least some people, and disable others – disappears behind this all-encompassing social construction, in which the virus itself is an 'invented' plague, as Agamben called it. But the proposed 'good biopolitics' challenge to this 'negative biopolitics', as called for by Benjamin Bratton in responding to Agamben, also falls short, glossing the specific impacts of Covid-19 – its peculiar biology: (very largely) respiratory spread, long latency periods, and large numbers of asymptomatic cases – and the interaction of those features with the institutions of capitalism. Instead, we are offered appeals to 'the responsibilities of medical knowledge' and the good of public health.

But knowledge doesn't have 'responsibilities': people in specific institutions facing specific situations do, with those specificities including the biological make-up of SARS-CoV-2 itself. There are hard limits on what our technologies can achieve because of these specificities, whether through vaccinations or the (more insidious) social technologies of control built into China's now-crumbling Zero Covid programme. Bratton's 'good biopolitics' isn't biological *enough*. Elsewhere, Panagiotis Sotiris has offered a 'democratic biopolitics' as an alternative to either 'plandemic' conspiracy theorising or lockdown fetishism. The recognition that a humane resolution – or even a route through – our multiple crises will require the active participation and engagement of the *demos* is to be strongly welcomed.

Covid-19 is neither a 'hoax' nor is it a generic medical emergency, to be treated separately from the society in which it arose by the good auspices of medical science. We know that Covid-19's health impacts are decisively shaped by pre-existing economic inequalities – the research lead by Michael Marmot for the UK is crystal clear on this. What has been perhaps less considered is the reverse causality: the prospect that Covid-19's uneven effects on capitalism are shaped by its public health impacts. Estimates for the specifically economic impacts of 'long covid' across the world vary, but are everywhere significant, including reduced numbers in work and direct costs to healthcare systems.

Our participation in the grand structures of capitalism has been radically disrupted by the virus, on a daily and continuous basis during the peak of lockdowns, and the form of that disruption to the structures – and therefore our agency – is intimately tied to the biological form of the virus that provoked it.

☭

Time in the pandemic

Most radical among these disruptions were the social distancing measures imposed from February 2020. The stasis of lockdown and then, creeping behind it, the radical, new uncertainty about the near future shattered otherwise well-rooted senses of the rhythm of the days, weeks and months, as psychological research is starting to show. We have, for generations now, operated in modern societies in accordance with a specific rhythm of work that appears as natural as the ebb and flow of the tides or the passing of the seasons, but which in reality had to be wrenched from the machines and then imposed on us all. Specific times on specific days were marked, too, by our physical locations: at the office or the factory during the week; at the home at the weekend. By disrupting that rhythm of place, forcing so many of us into furlough or working from home, the public health response to the pandemic has thrown open the organisation of the working day and the systems – from public transport to city centre sandwich shops – we built to sustain it.

But looking out beyond the disruption to long-established daily routines and we are peering as if into the mist. A future where covid continues to circulate, provoking disruptions – continued efforts at social distancing; longer-term health impacts – alongside the mushrooming of zoonotic spillovers and extreme weather events as climate change accelerates is one that is radically uncertain, relative to the recent past. Our best guides give us outlines of shapes, modelling the likely impacts of the virus into the future, but show nothing comparable to the stability that perhaps three generations have known, at least in the developed world, since the end of the Second World War – the last truly global disruption.

We are, of course, used to a degree of uncertainty in economic life: notoriously, capitalism is prone to booms and slumps, financial panics and manias, and a whole would-be social science (economics) is devoted to understanding them. Far more significant, however, than the volatility of the stock market, or even the ups and downs of the business cycle, is the profound *stability* of the capitalist economy underneath the froth: 'the movement of the whole disorder is its order', as Marx put it. It is the deep, stable structures of capitalism that attracted his interest: like other classical economists, his basic concern was how this incredibly unstable, decentred system could generate stability over time. By contrast, modern, neoclassical economics assumes stability, in the form of equilibrium, and then seeks to explain the deviations from this.

The classical economists' insight – that stability, rather than instability, is the fundamental that needs to be explained – may sound similar to that offered by the fashionable belief in the 'emergent properties' of systems, in which choices by individual actors – each following a more-or-less simple set of instructions – can spontaneously generate large-scale and persistent structures. The self-regulating systems of the natural world, in which the balances of predators to prey to sources of nutrition oscillate over time, but do not tip into chaos, are a striking example of how closed systems can generate cyclical stability. Even seemingly chaotic events – the regular outbreaks of naturally-occurring forest fires, for example – can form part of the self-regulating system. It is understandable that these sorts of self-stabilising processes have acted as a spur to the modelling of capitalist economies in which self-interest behaviours of individuals form cyclically stable structures.

But the stability exhibited by capitalism is different to the stability predicted by these modelling efforts. We don't just form stable structures, as if out of nowhere, from our self-interested actions: we cling, doggedly, to the structures we have, as providers of meaning and security. The working day, stabilised in industrialising northern Europe after the mid-nineteenth century and then exported across the globe, is one such structure attracting stabilising beliefs of this kind: for many of us, work isn't just valuable; the particular form of regular, systematic and money-directed work is a goal in itself, as Sarah Jaffe's *Work Won't Love You Back* surveys.

And we can think about and create new structures. The rhythms of industrial capitalism were imposed on us, smashing through customary beliefs about the pace and timing of work, the proliferation of feast days and holidays, and venerable unofficial traditions like that of 'Saint Monday' – brilliantly reconstructed by E P Thompson in his classic essay, 'Time, Work-discipline and Industrial Capitalism'. It was the Industrial Revolution, and the technologies it introduced, that radically altered perceptions and uses of time. The development of clock-time had taken place in the centuries beforehand, with the steady perfection of the clockwork mechanism from the fourteenth century onwards. Sundials, water-clocks and hourglasses had provided an approximate division of the day since ancient times, with shadow clocks referenced in Egyptian and Babylonian astronomy, dating their use from around 1500 BCE.

What the breakthrough of the mechanical escarpment allowed, following its appearance in Europe around 1300, was to replace naturally-occurring markers of time with a significantly more precise artificial mechanism – the regular ticking of the clock now able to mark out hours, and, by the 1500s, minutes and seconds. Clocks spread onto public buildings, notably churches, across the continent in the fourteenth century, replacing much older water clock displays. It became possible to create a new perception of time, changing it from its appearance as a natural marker in the day – sunrise, noon, and sunset, a subset of the bigger, natural divisions of the year into its seasons – and into known, precise and public regulator for human life, as Lewis Mumford's *Technics and Civilisation* argues.

But this public, regulated time – a formal and official organisation of the public life of the community, or at least its leading members located in the professions, engaged in trade, or maintaining ecclesiastical roles – remained quite distinct from the industrial capitalism that this basic rhythm shifts fundamentally. In his account, the first round of industrialisation was as much the separation of working life from the patterns of nature as it was the imposition of machinery. Malm shows how water-wheels, in the early nineteenth century, were more efficient than the competing technology of the steam engine – producing more at lower cost – but that by being tied to natural provision, in the form of water courses, they acted as a barrier to the full control of the production process that industrialised capital accumulation demanded. A steam engine could be operated consistently, day after day, hour after hour, with a supply of fossil fuel and – crucially – pliable labour. A waterwheel was more erratic and this, in turn, created a space where labour could still assert its own authority over the production process. Centralising production in the towns and cities of the Industrial Revolution created the ability for the new steam-powered factories to exploit fossil fuel transported into the cities, and to force a crude new factory discipline on the population. This was, in the early years, notoriously brutal: the maximisation of profits for individual factory owners appeared to demand the maximisation of the working day, with twelve- or fifteen-hour days becoming the norm in factory districts in the north of England by 1820.

The broad variety of tasks that pre-industrial or proto-industrial work could encompass, and the capacity of the worker to maintain some control over them – setting the pace on a handloom, for example – were broken by the monotony of the factory division of labour. It was only through political struggle and legislation that industrial capitalism was, through the nineteenth century, steadily humanised, the working week becoming standardised at five-and-a-half days in England by the end of the century, and the full two-day weekend increasingly common. This humanisation of capital laid the foundations for the political style and strategy we would now recognise as *reformism*: not the wholesale rejection, in the name of the workers, of capitalism, but the smoothing out of its rough edges. The struggle for the working day, then, is the foundation of social democratic and labour movement politics.

The establishment of this humanised capitalism produced its own backwash: by stabilising the core of the system, capitalist organisation could be more readily forced into the rest of the non-capitalist world, drawing greater and greater circles of humanity and nature into a rhythm of production determined by the economic activities of the imperial core. And on the other side, as the social reproduction theorists correctly insist, capitalist stabilisation rested upon on a non-capitalist sphere of household reproduction that, after an initial and radical disruption in the early years of industrialisation, was rapidly reorganised on strictly gendered lines – the male breadwinner, female caregiver household – even as important elements of 'life-making work', notably around education and healthcare, were themselves taken outside of the household through the development of the modern welfare state.

The creation of industrial capitalism meant the creation of a form of life in which the basic regulation of our existence – how we spent our time – was determined by social forces, rather than by nature. It has meant that where a pre-industrial work pattern concentrated its activities in the summer and autumn months, economic activity in half the world now typically peaks in the winter, shaped by Christianity and consumer spending. More recent research from the Grantham Institute cautiously suggests that higher levels of GDP, indicating greater development, are associated with a reduction in the seasonal impact of temperature on production – that is, modern economies become more productive the further removed they are from natural rhythms.

With more than half of humanity, for the first time in its history, now living in towns and cities, we are all increasingly detached from the underlying time of the seasons or even diurnal life, factory shift work and the twenty-four-hour city both operating independently of natural day and night. This *geography* of industrialised time, and the attachment of time to a specific organisation of space, appears in two forms: first, and more obvious, in the 'annihilation of distance through time' as transport and communications technology improved and the trading relationships of the global economy were built. The second, less often analysed in these terms but even more

fundamental, was the organisation of individuals' locations in relation to time: work was performed in one place, home life in another,
social life in a third: *metro, boulot, dodo* is a 'spatio-temporal fix' in
daily life, in Bob Jessop's phrase.

The earlier *environmental time*, which bound humanity through
its common, biological experience to the rhythms of nature, had
been replaced by a new, socially constructed *capitalist time*: at the
level of society, a new rhythm of life supplanting the pre-industrial
pattern of the seasons and, at the level of the individual, the working
day and the working week around which our lives have been organised. Urbanisation is, then, a necessary but not sufficient condition
for growth of this kind to occur, creating a regulated geographical
space of capitalist time from which labour can be drawn and stable,
geographically-located markets into which its products can be sold.
Published more than fifteen years ago, Mike Davis' *Planet of Slums*
looked to a future, already emerging then, where urbanisation
globally had run far ahead of capitalist productive activities.

☭

Long-run growth

This reorganisation of time and space had its own long-run
dynamic, breaking with the nature-determined cyclicality of the
past. Generalised economic growth – apparent from the 1850s,
measurable from the 1930s, systematic from the 1950s – is the
primary form taken by this capitalist opposition to cyclical, environmental time. Growth is necessarily cumulative, pushing back
against the cyclical time of agriculture with an expansion of commodities that is, in principle, infinitely extendible. Where cycles in
accumulation do appear, they are dominated by those induced in
a competitively-organised and exploitative economy: the business
cycle of recessions and booms, the cycles of capital investment, or
the still longer (and more contested) Juglar or Kondratieff cycles.
This distinctively capitalist process of removing ourselves from
the environment, founded on both the exploitation of time spent
in work and of the bounty of the natural world itself, has proved

immensely rewarding: the more that cyclical, environmental time can be squeezed out of human existence, the greater the potential for the creation of commodities in endlessly different forms and therefore for the accumulation of wealth. *Alienation*, from both our own humanity and from the natural world of which we are part, can be productive, as Marx's early writings suggest.

For a brief period, this expanding mechanism of alienated creativity and the steady extinction of environmental time has pro-duced exceptional riches: in the West, during the 'Golden Age' of the post-war boom, the commodity bounty produced by industrial capitalism was spread with unprecedented equality through their populations; in the East, and especially China, the entire century-long process in the West was radically condensed, and produced an exceptionally rapid move into a globalised version of modernity for an extraordinarily large number of people.

Although it is common to divide this period of widespread pros-perity following World War Two into two periods – the 'Keynesian' and the 'neoliberal', roughly divided at or around 1979 – from the longer-run perspective of accumulation against the environment, it is one long period marked by the labour market's reach being expanded across the globe, the growth of commodity production on an extraordinary scale, and the (strictly temporary) existence of an environmental 'sweet spot' in which the environmental costs imposed by industrial capitalism did not have to be borne by capitalist society in general. Localised environmental calamities occurred, of course – from crises of chemical poisoning to the loss of biodiversity to the rising preponderance of climate-related dis-asters. But a *generalised* calamity, sufficient to halt and disrupt the accumulation machine globally, did not occur.

Pandemics in the last two centuries could be hugely destruc-tive, just as they have been throughout history, but they did not fundamentally disrupt the functioning of global capitalism. The twentieth century saw three influenza pandemics, one of which, the so-called 'Spanish flu' of roughly 1918 to 1921, may have killed over 5 per cent of the world's population at the time, or around 100 million people. Yet it seems to have burned through society like a wildfire: enormously destructive as it swept along, but leaving the basic structures and institutions of society untouched. The HIV/AIDS pandemic is ongoing, having claimed 36 million victims (and rising) since the virus was first identified in the early 1980s. Its local economic impacts, where the disease has become endemic, have been significant, but not catastrophic – a further burden to add to the toxic legacy of colonialism in sub-Saharan Africa, but not a dramatic change in the economic course. Similarly endemic diseases, like malaria, have a similar set of impacts, reinforcing existing structural problems and imbalances. The burden of disease is terrible for humanity; the impact on capitalism, more limited. No pandemic in capitalism's comparatively short history has presented an authentically systemic challenge to its operations.

☭

Novelty

Until now. The novel coronavirus was not only new to humanity on its identification in early 2020. It has been utterly novel in its social impacts. SARS-CoV-2, and its proliferation of variants, has become a particularly unsettling new element in our existences not because of its inherent destructiveness – it can be deadly, but compared to, say, the Black Death or the ferocity of newer diseases like Ebola, it is significantly less deadly, even in the absence of medical interventions. The destructiveness lies in the precise way in which it interacts with the global capitalist economy and, in particular, disorders its primary institution, which is the institution of labour-time.

The specific economic damage caused by Covid-19, and the reason this will prove to be a permanent disruption in the operation of capital across the globe, relates directly to the biological characteristics of the virus itself, and their interaction with global capital: an infectious respiratory illness with an unusually high number of asymptomatic cases, a relatively small (but nonetheless alarmingly high) number of severe or fatal cases, and a pattern of infection (we now know) strongly driven by a limited number of 'super-spreader' events. In a world built around proximity in cities and international trade and travel, it should be no surprise the virus has spread so rapidly – and that attempts to contain it have proved so disruptive, driven by attempts to impose social distancing. Two previous novel coronaviruses, SARS and MERS, were contained, leading to some hubristic ruminations on the success of the 'post-Westphalian' disease control system by public health researchers like David Fidler; but in both those cases, the number of asymptomatic cases was far lower than Covid-19, and the infectious period far shorter. Both were easier to manage.

As industrialised agriculture continues to encroach on the animal reservoirs of novel diseases – while providing perfect hothouses for their mutation and zoonotic transfer, as shown in Rob Wallace's *Big Farms Make Big Flu* – and as climate change continues to shake up natural environments, we can expect more novel diseases to emerge. The rate of new disease emergence appears to have been increasing steadily for the past four decades. Those diseases successfully breaking out of their limited initial circulation, spreading widely in the human population, and becoming truly threatening to *capitalism* – as well as mere human life – are likely to be similar in their biology to Covid-19: easily transmitted via respiration, with many asymptomatic infections and long periods of infectiousness before any symptoms appear. They will be viruses, in other words, selected by evolution to succeed in a world economy that we have built around dense urban living, paid employment in dedicated workplaces, and mass, frequent, long-distance travel.

Covid-19, then, is a disease of capitalism: whatever its origins (although not certain, the most likely cause is zoonotic transfer from some prior animal host, most likely a bat), it would not now be on its way to endemicity in the human population without it also being keyed in to the structures of global capitalism. (The counterfactual makes this clear: a virus less well-adapted would not have spread so far; natural selection made sure it was SARS-CoV-2 that was most likely to break out and will, presumably, repeat the trick with a similar pathogen at some point in the future.)

Industrial capitalism was built on the creation of regimented, organised and managed labour, set *against* the pace and timing of work determined by nature, or workers, or both in concert. Covid-19 throws this global organisation by capital of labour against nature into disorder. To disrupt the labour process is to disrupt the entire system of production, and it is this disruption – rather than the more superficial drop in demand, a disorder in the system but one relatively easily patched up by governments – that guarantees the longevity of Covid-19's economic impacts. Once the virus is present, a volatile new element is introduced into human relationships. In particular, the ability of capital's owners to exercise control over the performance of work-time is weakened – at points in the last few years, very radically so, via lockdowns and social distancing. Either social distancing is enforced by public authorities (including border restrictions and other checks on movement), or significant expenditures are made to reduce its impact – for instance, in imposing a costly new testing regime, or spending on vaccination, or in dealing with the longer-term health impacts. Or, perhaps most horrifying of all for capital, labour itself can enforce the requisite social protection measures and learn to exploit greater control over its use. At the very least, the cost of *purchasing the control of labour* under these circumstances becomes rather higher.

But the outbreak has moved through its own rhythm: we have been bound, for nearly three years, to the inexorable logic of viral reproduction, tied to an exponential process that ripped through our societies, breaking it only with a significant force of collective action via the social distancing measures. The rapid production of effective vaccines, and their deployment, has already begun to reduce the vertiginous effects of the exponent in viral reproduction. Deaths and hospitalisations can be brought under control with an effective vaccine programme. However, while the vaccine limits its impact, it does not *remove* the virus, and the unevenness of the vaccines' distribution – a virtual guarantee in an unequal and competitive capitalist world economy – means flare ups and new variants remain a risk. The sequencing of these, and future such shocks, is not that of the business cycle, nor the seasons, nor even the great regulators of global climates like the El Niño Southern Oscillation. It represents something new.

☭

The new time

This is crucial: the temporality of the virus itself is not tied to either still-familiar natural rhythms nor to those social rhythms we have created ourselves. A strange new kind of naturalism has appeared with the virus: with respiratory illness circulating more easily indoors, the retreat to indoor warmth in the winter months creates a distinctive seasonality to the progress of Covid-19 itself, much as flu and other more common illnesses flare up during the winter. We find ourselves, for a while, in something resembling a hibernation cycle, or at least an economic existence brought closer to the agricultural seasons: firing up the re-vaccination programme in the winter while reintroducing some elements of social distancing and depressing some kinds of economic activity, just as winter was a dead time in the past. Unlike the four other, more tame coronaviruses in common circulation among humans, SARS-CoV-2 is 'aggressive': it cannot be easily managed on a seasonal basis because it mutates easily and, even in milder forms, is highly virulent for at least some cases. As epidemiologist Jeffrey Sharman has noted, the patterns of covid's eruption are, so far, more disorderly than those of existing endemic diseases like seasonal influenza.

Looking ahead, as older diseases resurge, as antibiotic resistance spreads, and as new diseases make their journey from animal hosts to humanity – the latest, Langya henipavirus, was identified as causing respiratory conditions in eastern China in August 2022 – the shape of the future perhaps begins to become clearer. Having created the space where a combination of effective medicines and effective public health had held back what disease researcher Amesh Adhilja called the 'horde of pathogens' that had 'killed us at will' for most of our history, the future is one in which the effective technologies remain in place – witness the extraordinarily rapid success of the vaccine – but their use is conditioned by a society subject to repeated, disastrous shocks. The defences of the last two hundred years, during which industrial capitalism established itself, are set to be breached, repeatedly. We lack the social capacity and organisation to prevent it. Attempts to construct those defences, through state action and willpower alone, merely mutate the crisis at great social cost: each fresh lockdown in China's industrial heartlands contributes to supply-chain disruptions across the globe.

We are confronted by the old, natural seasonality, brought back in industrialised form: it is the alienated reappearance of a changed nature in our social existence; the blowback, with covid as the first of many such shocks, from two centuries of industrialised capital accumulation now reappearing as ecological decline. How we experience this ecological descent, including its temporality, is mediated through the appearance of novel diseases and other lingering calamities: these are not distinct from the descent; they *are* the descent, as we experience it.

We do not see climate change as such: its temporality is all wrong from the viewpoint of either the individual or society. But we see its impacts, and these impacts are cumulative. The environment itself reimposes historical, accumulated time on our actions. Just as capital is erected as a barrier against the forces of time itself – it is the accumulation of dead, spent labour and consumed, utilised nature, organised in a hierarchy – so too is the toll of extraction against the environment eventually becoming an immense cost extracted against capital itself. Time will have its revenge.

But what we are threatened with is not a return to a pre-industrial environmental time, but a *new form of capitalist time*: one where the regulation of human life is no longer under the purview of capital, and subject to its specific pace, but one where human life is bound by the mediated re-emergence of the environment. Further novel diseases are virtually guaranteed, and the very success of Covid-19 strongly indicates the future forms they could take that will be most disruptive.

But worsening extreme weather, food shortages, disruptions to the supply of essential commodities: all of these help turn the human economy from nature's master to its servant. That, in turn, strongly suggests that the great engine of industrial growth, running for the last two centuries, will no longer function so effectively.

If capitalism cannot easily make objects out of labour and nature, it cannot easily produce the exchange values that it registers as growth. In less abstract terms, the costs of production increase with environmental decay, and so do the difficulties of *control* and *management* of production. To ease the latter, states across the world will be dragged increasingly into the productive process itself – organising supply chains, providing funding, and offering their services for the monitoring and surveillance of labour.

Covid-19, then, is not a 'crisis' in the usual sense: it represents something closer to a semi-permanent state of existence. The epidemiological modelling points towards the virus becoming endemic and, with luck and effective vaccines, it will become – if not entirely harmless – at least less obviously unstable and destructive over the next few years. But a decade-long state of existence is not, by the usual standards, a 'crisis'. It is how the world actually is: a marker of the ecological decay we are living through – and the first of many such shocks and disruptions. It points us to a future where similar such shocks impact our society in broadly similar ways, the precise vectors of the shock depending crucially on the biological parameters of the diseases in question. The 'first crisis of the Anthropocene' is the last of the ordered, capitalist world we have known.

GARGI BHATTACHARYYA

The Arse-End of Empire at the Arse-End of the World

Britain no longer feels invulnerable. This is a coming together of global unsettlement in the face of ecological collapse and the unhappy realisation of the everyday hardship and dysfunction of life in a (differently) collapsing Britain. People do still try to resurrect some old refrains. Fifth largest economy in the world (not any more) – often reframed as fifth richest society (nothing like). But people have lost their belief in Britain's ability to be cushioned against the troubles of the world.

The attempt to 'make Britain great again' came forty years before Trump, a refrain of the Thatcher years and sewn into that government's toxic concoction of petty nationalism, enforced scarcity, union-busting and reinvigorated racism. We might reflect, with hindsight, on what that project of resurrecting 'greatness' set in motion. For all the talk about aspiration, and the reams of analysis devoted to understanding the Thatcherite hegemonic project, perhaps in the end it is the training to tolerate hardship that stands as Thatcherism's longest shadow.

Liz Truss tripping over her own feet as she awkwardly stumbles into the royal funeral flicks a switch in global consciousness. More even than Boris, Truss reflected the world's view of us. Delusional to the point of inducing pity, a spectacle that would be funny if it were not so very dangerous. When empires finally die, it will be farcical.

But the farce is not in the personalities involved. The sticking plaster of an imposed Sunak does little to dispel the sense of decline and unfolding chaos. The put-on seriousness of Jeremy Hunt (who must be more surprised than anyone to be feted as a person competent in anything) announces the necessity to push down living standards more and more sharply than ever before – and, on the whole, the national response from all sides has been little more than technical. The renewed militancy across the labour movement is constrained by anti-union laws that outlaw 'political disputes', leaving union spokespeople struggling to explain their sectoral claims without straying into any more general analysis of Britain's malaise, lest the law is used to immobilise their union and its funds.

The jokes about nothing working are already decades old and internationally known. British plumbing? Ha ha ha. Transport? Dental health? Queues and bureaucracy and every system large and small. Britain has been known for a practised inefficiency. For a while, it was possible to sneer at the unsightly urgency of, say, Americans. Or the humourless smooth running of German institutions and businesses. For a lot of years, Britain spun out the role of aristocratic decline, genteel but down-at-heel, but since 2008 there has been an escalation in the depth and reach of decline. This is not about some fiction of status on the world stage. It is about the grim deprivation that features in so many, too many, unremarked lives.

I have to admit that 2022 was energising. What next, what next? For a moment, it did seem that we were witnessing the implosion of the political class. And it still feels as if no-one wants the reins of power. There is a weak continuation of electoralism, but without much content. Austerity is revamped with the Tory defence going no further than the assertion that it is Putin not Truss who is to blame.

Ⴚ

It can be quite hard to think of a politics that does not revolve around versions of messaging. Even traditions which foreground the science of socialism tend towards a belief in the power of well-expressed reason. We think, most of the time, that we are engaging our enemies on the terrain of ideas and that our task is to win hearts, minds and arguments. This, we believe, is how political consciousness works and we rely on the weight of our explanatory narrative to carry our politics. Most of all, we act as if being able to explain how bad things happened makes us seem the most likely candidates for making something better happen next.

The observation that critique is not the same thing as vision or rebuilding has become banal. But I wonder if this moment, when the arse-end of empire comes fully into view, demands a reassessment of our collective political habits. In particular, the implied sequencing of ideas, communication and organisation – with critique of the ugliness of the world leading to political speech to persuade others of the unethical basis of this ugliness leading, we hope, to the altered consciousness that brings people to us. And then? Well, amass the numbers and victory will follow. Isn't that secretly what we hope and believe?

Do not mistake this for an argument to return to civil discourse or a rebuilding of the public sphere or any form of return to some lost former state of grace. In light of what we understand about the pervasive scepticism of our time, we might need to consider the challenges of building any politics in the face of such widespread distrust and scepticism. The simultaneous opening of the public square and fragmenting of collective bonds creates spiralling questions in response to all and any attempts to shape what people think.

We grasp that someone or something is trying to cheat us. How could we not? But it is quite hard to discern the alliances of the powerful in a house on fire.

Ⴚ

When former powers collapse, it is a slow-motion affair.

We all laugh, with a gallows humour, about the shit in the sea off Britain's beaches. One highly visible outcome of Brexit has been the ability of British water companies to pump untreated sewage directly into the seas off the coast.

There are warnings of planned power cuts to regulate the energy supplies through the winter. There is some outcry, a little, mainly from predictable quarters. Mainly the breakneck speed of 'events' in British political life takes up everyone's attention. There is insufficient bandwidth for people to consider too much what might happen next, because the energies required to process and survive what is happening right now leave us depleted.

I think this, too, is a tactic of power.

However, this cultivated inattention may no longer be sustainable. The over-focus on the spectacle of collapse risks a non-understanding of the machinery of collapse and how this particular moment and mode of collapse impacts on our lives.

At the risk of stating the painfully obvious, the performance of political life is not necessarily in sync with the fragmentation of infrastructure. Some of what occurs as the arse-end of empire is revealed does not pass through the 'public square' or the 'battle of ideas' at all.

Perhaps the incompetence of the political class is a cause for ridicule and entertainment. Perhaps the theatre of political life revolves around the critiques and promises of some better machinery of distribution and administration.

But what is collapsing around us is beyond any time-limited policy battle. What is in motion is the reckoning of decades of slower decline, neglect and an unavoidable fall from dominance. Perhaps this is a reckoning with national structures which could not be sustained except from a position of dominance (and I know various important interventions have made the case that public infrastructure in Britain is another spoil of coloniality, reflecting the injection of stolen resources and wealth).

Perhaps because belatedly, there is considerable energy put into uncovering the colonial underpinning of the welfare state and pretty much all aspects of the social wage as it has existed in Britain. Although unarguable as an insight, my sense is that we are still feeling our way through the implications of this (until recently repressed) knowledge. The claims of both the electoral and the street left in Britain have revolved around the assertion that there is enough for all and it is class theft that causes our pain, not any limit of resources.

Worlding our understanding of British welfarism unsettles that framing, beyond repair I suspect. We learn, rightly, that the social wage is funded via the legacy and continuation of colonial violence. Alongside this, welfarism has been motored by the parallel narratives of entitlement (cradle to grave) and national family (pride of Britain). The publicly owned and/or administered infrastructure of everyday life has been the ground on which the terms of belonging are played out. The National Health Service has held a talismanic role in this melding of symbolism and material practice, for obvious reasons, but we might consider whether the celebration of a socialised health service is also a cipher for something more. Perhaps not quite a celebration of the role of state, but certainly an acceptance that some greater authority must be in place to administer this scale of collective resources. Bordering has operated as the violent and deadly mechanism by which access to social goods and to a wider terrain of the means of life are rationed, but, simultaneously, there has been a roundabout embrace of state-administered infrastructure. The odd doublethink of (post?)imperial consciousness has been characterised by this tension between exclusion and mutuality, between collectivism and exceptionalism, between ideas of togetherness and the celebration of ourselves alone.

☭

To understand the arse-end of empire, we must shift our gaze away from the spectacle of representation. We must think a little less about what is said or how it is said. And a little more about the collapsing infrastructure of places where the cumulative impact of asset-stripping makes it difficult to maintain what is needed to sustain life.

The drip drip drip of hardship is a hegemonic technique. Disciplining bodies and ensuring that much of our lives are spent trying to survive, to look after our loved ones, to fix and mend and make do, to juggle bills and keep things afloat. Making everyday life hard is a way of 'shaping the debate'. It is a way of making sure that most people do not have the time or energy to pay too much attention to the details of corruption or dishonesty or theft from above. But it is also a way of breaking our spirits just enough to pass as consent. Years of arguing for our rights as a common good, with the quiet assumption that economic growth is good for us all, have muted our memory of the role of enforced hardship as a technique of domination.

But, in yet another painful irony, enforced hardship as a technique of government has been familiar across colonised spaces. We know too well that colonial powers operated through extreme violence, undertaking torture, rape, mutilation, murder and genocide in the name of civilisation, progress or just plain profit.

But also the impossibility of ease, the rationing of all human comforts. The wilful squeezing of living standards is also a kind of hegemonic project. Hardship also shapes political consciousness and not necessarily as resistance, whatever we may wish. Official neglect and institutional collapse force people into time-hungry processes to preserve life. The extensive efforts needed to chase down the right medication or to queue to access the necessary service or to identify the next gatekeeper in attempts to navigate what remains of public services and/or avoid the punitive sanctions of failing to follow systems which operate erratically as they collapse all remake political consciousness. Exhaustion can limit our horizons or attention to the powerful. Critique feels like an inappropriate register to gather people being broken by life.

☭

Much of the world understands all too well what is happening in Britain. Some have traced these steps themselves in earlier times.

Others have waited generations for this promised revenge, and now dare not speak too soon in case the chance is lost.

Life in the former imperial metropolis reveals an accelerating collapse, with social relations being remade on the hoof and, sometimes, in scary ways. This moment for Britain – the moment when life gets much harder very quickly, when institutional forms erode to near disappearance and when few political formations seem close to being fit for the purpose of bringing us together or illuminating the place we are in (I hold off judgement on whether the heartening resurgence of trade unions can instigate this last need) – is dangerous but unspectacular. And in the grey grind of trying to make do and survive, monsters can and do appear.

There is a temptation to try to end with a flourish, isn't there? Denunciation is always good copy. If there is denunciation needed, surely we are among those to be denounced. Any defence of access to the social goods being stripped away runs so close to a defence of things 'as they were'. Perhaps the small gains of welfare and healthcare and employment regulation grappled from the grasping hands of the British ruling class through struggle and (let us say it quietly) a very brief experiment with social democracy are tainted as exclusionary benefits delimited by nation. In a parallel to the paradox of claims made on stolen land, there is a question about any defence of social goods eroded or at risk as a result of imperial collapse. Surely those benefits were never legitimately 'ours' in the first place. Or, at least, not ours alone. The world does not see our pain, they see our comeuppance.

I don't want to overplay it. Most people in Britain will eat, just a bit less, cutting nutritional corners. People have been learning to do this since the 2008 crash, so not a new emergency. Everyone shares making do and mend stories, putting on their extra jumpers, with baked potatoes in their pockets and hot water bottles on their feet. Some of the old and vulnerable die every winter, so nothing to write home about as we all get a bit colder. Public services have been stretched for fifteen years, gradually slicing out provision until only the bare bones (or less) survive across all essential services. Healthworkers issue stark warnings about the imminent collapse of the health service and the place of this concocted crisis in the service of moving to some or other variety of private insurance model of healthcare provision. Ambulances do not arrive. The elderly lie on the floor screaming with pain for hours, hoping paramedics will arrive sometime. Teachers fill their desk drawers with snacks, hoping to sneak enough calories to hungry children for everyone to get through the day. The old and the young and the displaced and the unlucky will keep on dying and we will keep on acting as if such deaths are accidental.

I have nothing else to say. It is arse. But it is the end.

JAMIE ALLINSON

Fossil Sovereignty and Anthropocene Freedom

The following is based on a contribution to Salvage's *panel, 'Freedom in the Twenty-first Century', at the 2022 Historical Materialism conference in London.*

I. The prospect of ecological collapse and the reassertion of natural limits to growth – or even the programme of de-growth – pose severe challenges to a Marxist politics of freedom. Such a politics has long been premised on the idea of an actually-existing collective abundance that would emancipate individuals from the blind operation of forces external to them. Bourgeois freedom, by contrast, consists of the liberation of individuals from personal domination only to subject them to the general domination of such external forces. This is the 'abstract domination', as described in Moishe Postone's *Time, Labor and Social Domination*, of scarcity and the compulsion to sell one's labour-power. For bourgeois freedom, prosperity is the outcome; for proletarian freedom, abundance is the precondition.

Were a proletarian revolution to succeed in any currently conceivable timescale – in itself a remote proposition – its primary task would be to reverse, or at least modify, the process of growth in order to preserve minimum conditions of habitability. This would imply the transition to forms of power-generation that do not rely on burning fossil fuels and preferably not on the consumption of non-renewable sources of energy in general.

What then is the relationship between energy transition and freedom? And what are the implications of this relation not just for the abolition of currently existing structures of domination, exploitation and oppression but for the prospects of collective emancipation?

This is far too large a question for one essay. What I will try to do here instead is to pose it in a Marxist way, to see if that is useful not just to the project of human survival but of human freedom. Rather than tackle the relationship between the terms, energy transition and collective freedom, in a conceptual way, we must look historically at how bourgeois forms of freedom, of both property and labour, have been intertwined with energy transitions. This is not (just) because these are necessarily examples for a future transition, but because they are the historical preconditions for the present: the point at which we have now arrived and from which any future transition would necessarily be launched.

The starting point lies with Marxist accounts of freedom and where energy transition fits into them, or not – which may also be related to other gaps within such accounts. What I want to explore here is an intuition, as yet no more than that, that they are connected.

☭

II. For Marxists, 'freedom' is not a transhistorical or cross-class value. It belongs to certain historical circumstances, to certain modes of production, and has certain characteristics according to its expression of the class interests generated by those modes of production.

For this reason, Marxist accounts of the history of contemporary freedom are accounts of the origins of bourgeois freedom, including the freedom enjoyed by proletarians under the capitalist mode of production (that is to say, the bourgeois freedom of the worker). These debates therefore revolve around the nature and history of what Marx calls the 'dual freedom' of the direct labourer, which is what makes a proletarian.

Dual freedom means that the proletarian is divested of the coercive control of a particular person over them, but also divested of the means of production by which they can reproduce themselves. Free to choose, and free to lose; free to work and free to starve. The process by which Marx argues this separation occurred – elaborated upon in chapter nine of the first volume of *Capital* – is one aspect of 'primitive accumulation'. As the labourer is divorced from the means of labour, labour power is transformed into a commodity, the exchange of which is then co-ordinated on the market. This process is central to the formation of capital as a relationship between exploiter and exploited.

The other aspect of primitive accumulation is the accumulation of capital as a stock – a history 'written in letters of blood and fire' – through slavery and colonial loot amongst other things. Both of these aspects may have a connection to energy transition.

Before exploring this possibility, however, it is important to note that primitive accumulation has formed the starting point for Marxist accounts of freedom because it is the story of the emancipation of 'free labour', and 'free labour' is the necessary counterparty of capital.

From this account of freedom comes the influential idea that non- or pre-capitalist societies are characterised by specific relations of personal domination (even if their ideological categories of religious belief, caste or hereditary relationships, are abstractions in the sense of not referring to particular people), whereas capitalism is characterised by abstract domination. This is a shared baseline across otherwise very different Marxist thinkers such as Ellen Wood, Postone, Derek Sayer, Heide Gerstenberger and others, although they diverge from that baseline in terms of how they characterise and study capitalism, and its associated forms of political power.

There are several problems here with what 'domination' means and who is subjected to it, but these can be left aside for now. More important is the implication of this argument for the contradictory nature of bourgeois freedom. That implication, as drawn out in the German state derivation debates of the 1970s, is that there is something different about the capitalist state that implies the defence of property in general.

The capitalist state-form, unlike the feudal or, as I prefer, tributary state, is not just the victory of one group of exploiters over others in a hierarchical relation but the coordination mechanism by which all exploiters may compete with each other without the system tearing itself apart. This then implies the defence of all forms of property. That is to say, the capitalist state, then, defends not only particular properties or property holders but all forms of property. It is this that makes the capitalist state capitalist, not that capitalists run it.

This is also what distinguishes 'republican' ideas of liberty from liberal accounts of freedom. But as Andrew Sartori in *Empire and Liberalism* and Aaron Jakes in *Egypt's Occupation: Colonial Economism and the Crises of Capitalism* both note, this introduces a contradiction into the bourgeois conception of freedom. The property owner of labour power – the worker – is accorded the same freedom, at least formally, as the owner of property in the means of production. Hence the formal neutrality of the bourgeois state, which is always riven by this contradiction.

There are some problems with this account. First of all, its apparent indifference to actually-existing capitalist states, which are frequently run not just for but by identifiable groups of capitalists. Second, the apparent taking at face value of the bourgeois state's claim that it is neutral and separate from society, or that it doesn't subject labour to direct domination. This leads onto the most powerful objection: that in both its genesis and its operation the capitalist mode of production has been constitutively dependent on unfree, violently dominated labour-power. The distinction between free and unfree labour has not just coincided with but formed the substance of the social practice known as 'race'. This has operated either at the level of individual un-freedom, or rather the making of a category of un-individuals who can then be perpetually unfree, or at the collective level, through the denial of sovereignty in the form of colonisation.

I will return to this point. First I want to add another one, which I think is connected: the absence in the Marxist account of dual freedom of the actual operation of power. By this I mean not political, ideological or social power but physical power: the generation and transmission of energy to do work. Why, and how, might these be connected?

☭

III. In the past two decades, the flourishing of eco-socialist scholarship has begun to re-introduce the physical generation of power into this account of capitalist transition. As with the debate on dual freedom and abstract versus personal domination, or economic versus extra-economic coercion, I will not survey all of the individual contributions but rather establish a baseline claim among them. That baseline is the necessity of fossil fuels for the rift in the social metabolism with nature that produces and reproduces human life. But why might this be connected to primitive accumulation and dual freedom? And what could that connection be?

The answer to this question lies in a key argument in Andreas Malm's *Fossil Capital*. Malm's claim is that different sources of energy allow for different social relations of production. He distinguishes between flow (wind, water, sunshine); animate (muscle power, animals); and finally stock (fossil, coal, oil, although perhaps nuclear power would come into this too). Energy as stock allows for full subsumption of the labour process. Industrialisation in England and Scotland from the turn of the eighteenth century occurred because it allowed the class power of the capitalist to be exercised in the production process rather than something dependent upon the flow of wind or water power, not under their control.

In Malm's account, energy transition is thus mapped onto the shift between formal and real subsumption, which historically occurred after the separation of labour from the means of production, and therefore the 'economy', in England at least. There may still be a connection, however, in the following ways. First of all: the initial burst of deforestation that occurred in England in the fifteenth-seventeenth centuries. Some of Marx's earliest writings, collected in Daniel Bensaïd's edited volume *The Dispossessed*, concern the so-called 'wood theft' debates in Prussia about the assertion of land-owners' (newly established) 'rights' to property in the fallen wood on their land which peasants customarily gathered for fuel.

In England, and to some extent in Scotland, deforestation (for fuel and for ship- and housebuilding) did coincide with enclosures; the separation of the labourer from the means of production. In fact, coal began to be widely used for heating and fuel in England in the late sixteenth and early seventeenth century because of an 'energy crisis' caused by the shortage of wood. Wood is a renewable resource – the forest is allowed to grow back – but in other ways it is a stock, since it is moveable and also exhaustible once a forest has been chopped down.

Animate and flow energy is topographically limited. It is uneven in its distribution in certain sites and therefore the exploitative accumulation of a surplus from it requires – outside of a marketed portion – going to that site of production or compelling, ideologically or physically, the producers to render some of their production from it. That is to say, personal domination or what Ellen Wood calls 'extra-economic' coercion. Stock fuel, as Malm notes, allows for formal subsumption, industrialisation, and urbanisation. That means control by the capitalist, but it also means the exploited comes to the exploiter. Cities and towns are much harder places in which to enforce coercive, unbounded exploitation because people can run away and find other options. This is one reason why people move to them, and so many have – either in their own countries of origin or through migration to other cities around the world.

Moreover, stock, again as Malm shows, provides the basis for abstract labour time (which is key to Postone's argument, for example). The wage relation conceals the exploitation that direct coercive or personal domination, based on flow or animate energy, reveals.

☭

IV. These may not be historically defensible claims. There are some large objections. The most obvious ones are to do with the previously mentioned point about the prominence of unfree, and also unwaged, labour, in both the genesis and perpetuation of capital accumulation. And indeed, until the nineteenth century in Scotland at least, coal miners were not free – they wore collars bearing the amount of reward available for their return to their master if they ran away. Scottish collieries in fact only stopped using formally unfree labour about thirty years earlier than British plantations in the New World did. The role of unfreed labour, in New World slavery and other forms, was more consequential in providing calorific inputs to metropolitant labour power. The other place that happened or happens, of course, is in the unwaged private domain of the household.

These objections suggest the need to return to the connection between full emancipation – personal and abstract – under communism and energy transition. I have suggested there may be a connection between the dual freedom and abstract domination of capitalism, and forms of energy as stock. Would there be, or is there reason to talk about there being, such a connection between renewable energy sources and abstract emancipation?

My initial answer is that there is no necessary connection because, first of all, renewable forms of energy generation are still quite significant pieces of the means of production, especially at the scale required, say, to run a public transport system. Second, even if the primary capture of the energy were to take the form of a flow, its storage in, for example, batteries, would act like a stock.

Nonetheless, there might be a different way of looking at this if we consider the nature of proletarian un-freedom. In a 1985 essay, 'On the Structure of Proletarian Unfreedom', G A Cohen identifies the nature of proletarian unfreedom as consisting of the collective fact of the compulsion to sell one's labour power. Even if every individual proletarian were swapped for another individual, making the first a bourgeois, there must exist such a group of proletarians in order for capital accumulation to continue. The condition of the freedom of any given proletarian, or finite group of proletarians, is the continuing compulsion of the others. Hell is other people.

If that compulsion were abolished then capitalism would be abolished, which indeed is precisely the prospectus that we favour. Yet this argument implies a further condition: that levels of production are sufficient for the compulsion not to arise. Notice, however, that sufficient is not the same as abundant, or rather only abundant relative to an established standard of living.

This leads to the following points. The first is that renewable energy is certainly capable of meeting that level of relative abundance or sufficiency: not luxury communism but adequate enough for proletarian freedom. The second point, however, is that even though, once established, the marginal costs of renewable generation tend to zero, this is not enough on its own to change the distribution of property relations needed to abolish proletarian unfreedom. We can no more expect any putative green capitalism to pass over into eco-socialism than we could have expected fossil-fed industry to evolve into twentieth-century communism.

RICHARD SEYMOUR

Freedom on a Damaged Planet

The following is based on a contribution to Salvage's *panel, 'Freedom in the Twenty-first Century', at the 2022 Historical Materialism conference in London.*

'The history of the world is nothing but the development of the idea of freedom' – Hegel

I. Freedom in the twenty-first century is freedom in an ecologically damaged world. One of the first crises of freedom in the twenty-first century came in the form of an ecological crisis, a global pandemic likely sparked by the zoonotic leap of a Covid-19 virus from the wildlife reservoir. But what are we calling freedom?

Freedom is a powerful myth of capitalist modernity, especially petromodernity. And, being allied to capitalist growth, this is mainly a negative freedom: freedom from interference in voluntary contracts. Any policy that could restrict growth, by restraining the right of individuals to strike whatever contracts they see fit – buying an airline ticket, or buying an airline – would appear to be counter-freedom.

There is another conception of freedom linked to the social-ist, feminist and anti-racist freedom struggles, which has more in common with the republican tradition described by Quentin Skin-ner: political freedom from domination. This isn't to be confused with abolition or emancipation, though political freedom has been driven up the agenda by Black Lives Matter, anti-carceral and anti-police struggles. Freedom, as Foucault pointed out, is what comes after emancipation. As I've said before, just because you decapitate the king doesn't mean you've abolished the monarchy.

Now this shows that freedom is inherently a partisan matter. Marxism is a form of thought, a critical procedure, that tries to free humanity from 'the realm of necessity'. And, because in that way it's a form of practical knowledge, it can't accept a simple distinction between fact and value, is and ought. So when Marxists talk about freedom, as Lenin repeatedly insisted, we immediately face the question: freedom for whom, and for what purposes? There's a despotic potential in such questions, if it results in nothing but contempt for liberal freedoms (as in Lenin's reported response, in 1920, to Men-shevik critics: 'Of course, gentlemen, you have all the freedom to publish this critique – but, then, gentlemen, be so kind as to allow us to line you up the wall and shoot you!') But that doesn't mean we can avoid the problem. And it has become more urgent now that it's clearer that the realm of necessity is going to outlast capitalism.

𝒢

II. The animating myth of capitalist freedom derives its power from various concrete, unequal freedoms. Take the freedom of movement. I have the freedom to fly from London to New York, as long as I have enough money. That freedom doesn't exist for those who have the wrong passport, or are politically stigmatised, or could never dream of having enough money, because it is realised in institutional (market and state) forms that congeal unequal access to the resources of petromodernity. That makes it contestable. Either it should be universal, or maybe I should not have that freedom, or maybe it should be rationed.

During the height of the Covid-19 pandemic, the freedom to travel between states (and often out of your home) was seriously abridged in order to limit the spread of a virus that has officially killed 6.6 million people worldwide. You can legitimately argue over whether that was necessary given the scale of the crisis, the alternatives, the trade-offs and so on. But if you dispute that it could ever be necessary, that seems to place a very high price on my freedom to travel. It trumps, in principle, all the freedoms of those who might die as a result of my transmitting the disease. What politics of class and race does that assume? You could argue that restricting the right to travel is racist, or at least racially laden, and liable to punish migrants and refugees more than the business and tourism travellers who constitute the majority of such flows. But, obviously, so would allowing the disease to spread, since we all acknowledge that racism and poverty are pre-existing health conditions. I can see no intelligent way for anyone on the Left to argue against such coercion in principle.

Now take another example. Should my freedom to travel by plane be removed, or at least rationed, to limit carbon emissions? As a matter of current technological necessity, flying causes world-destroying emissions. One can minimise these – air travel 'only' causes 2.5 per cent of all emissions – but that 2.5 per cent still counts given how close we are to exhausting the carbon 'budget'. So if you say that such restrictions are not reasonable in principle, you're once more putting a very high price on the freedom for the estimated 4 per cent of the world's population who take international flights. This figure conceals inequalities. For example, while the average person in the US is said to emit a total of seven metric tons of CO_2 annually, the owners of private jets have emitted on average 3,300 metric tons from those jets alone. Further, the profitable core of the airline industry is business travellers – members of a growing transnational capitalist class involved in finance, tech and global governance. Still, most flights are for leisure, or to see family.

How many might lose all freedom for this to continue? A pandemic is a relatively discrete event, in which deaths are measurable. Is it possible to safely measure how many will die of drought, flooding, storms, overheating, wildfires and the decimation of the food chain in the coming years? Probably not with any precision, but we can't make big political decisions without at least some sort of idea. According to a recent study, extreme weather currently accounts for 9.4 per cent of global deaths each year, which is about 5 million people. Not all of this is driven by climate change. But it's a reasonable inference that as extreme weather becomes more recurrent, it will account for a lot more death worldwide.

So let's have some bids: how many more excess deaths triggered by this single variety of ecological disaster is worth the uninhibited right to fly? Five million? Ten million? Remember, it's good and edifying to be well-travelled, there are places to see, families to visit, cultures to experience. I hear twenty million: can I get fifty million? How much of other people's freedom and flourishing, and our own in future, shall we, the 4 per cent, burn?

☭

III. The pandemic is a good place to start for exploring this question of what freedom might look like on a damaged planet.

While the image we get from neoliberal ideology is that we are always managing the risks that others represent to us, the plague is one situation in which we acknowledge ourselves as the bearers of risk. Wherever we go, we bring the grim reaper with us. Take a sneaky holiday to Cornwall in April 2020, and you may well have been bringing them the plague. 'Act Like You've Got It, Anyone Can Spread It', the British government announced in its ad campaigns. We are all unclean, no one is innocent.

Now I'm not here to defend lockdown per se – I think a pro- or anti-lockdown position is fundamentally beside the point. But the fact that our risk is not simply of becoming ill, but of killing others, was tellingly elided in so much anti-lockdown eristic – though it is essential to any egalitarian ethics.

One anti-lockdown argument that didn't completely evade this essential problem was Panagiotis Sotiris' analysis for *Historical Materialism*. I don't wholly agree with it, as will become clear, but it raises profound questions that should interest us if we're serious about building freedom on a damaged planet. Crucially, Sotiris is looking for alternatives to capitalist biopolitics, to the surveillance, control and regimentation of populations by medical bureaucrats and national governments. As he points out, in a way lockdown – though justified in terms of social solidarity – purges disease control of its social and political content. Lockdown strategies contain no acknowledgment of pre-existing health conditions like racism and poverty. Although leading anti-lockdown reactionaries criticised it for disrupting their normal – that is, exclusive, partisan – freedoms, actual lockdown strategies far more severely compound the existing unfreedoms experienced by the working class and racially oppressed, and indeed by anyone who might experience the wrong end of a police baton.

So, Sotiris – in a way that I think is actually premature, or prefigurative – tries to discern a possible democratic or communist biopolitics. He references the history of ACT UP, which offered medical help for AIDS sufferers during that pandemic amid callous, homophobic official indifference. He references the Black Panthers' 'survival pending revolution' strategy. One might add the brief flourishing of mutual aid in the early days of the pandemic. What he's referencing here is what we sometimes call 'self-help'. What Foucault in his study of ancient philosophers calls 'the care of the self'. Which is not about scented candles and feng shui, but about the conditions necessary for citizenship, for living freely. We cannot be free if we don't take care of ourselves – that is, if we don't understand who we are, what we desire, what we are capable of – because we will misuse ourselves and others. We will be what the philosopher Harry Frankfurt calls 'wantons', easy meat for purveyors of exploitation, addictive products, sleazy disinfotainment, and so on. And that makes us irresponsible. To partake of social being, as Marx called it, we need to be capable of reorienting our willpower, of achieving more conscious control over our desires. A communist biopolitics asks you to do that: self-isolate if you need to, we will help; stay off work if you need to, we will provide; if you need company, we will try to give it within our means: but, comrade, you must take care of yourself. Just as you might need a partner or a parent to take care of themselves, we need each other to take care of ourselves.

But I agree with Gareth Dale's retort. Lockdown unarguably brings evils, but so do the alternative strategies (test-trace-isolate), and so does the spread of Covid-19. And even if you think this pandemic didn't necessitate centralised, top-down biopolitical controls – and I really disagree with you or at least insist that you outline your predicates, your costing, your analysis of who benefits and who dies – but setting that aside, even if we agree to say that this pandemic didn't necessitate such coercion, you should at least admit that other pandemics, and other ecological emergencies, could do so. That, while there is a legitimate struggle over how funds and resources are distributed, how coping mechanisms are embedded in communities, and who pays the costs of preparedness and disease control, localised responses lacking the direct coercive element and scaling of big public monopolies may not be enough. After all, we are by and large committed to handling ecological crisis and class justice by means of global planning. However democratic and egalitarian that may be, it seems foolish to me to think we are ever going to eliminate coercion and injustices entirely, however much the iron fist is sheathed in the velvet glove.

☭

IV. Marxism is nothing if not a tragic vision of human history. For the vast majority of human existence, it argues, nothing has been possible apart from poverty and unfreedom for the majority. Socialist freedom, as freedom from the realm of necessity, freedom for the majority and not just a ruling class from the exigencies of survival, only seriously comes on the agenda once the freak occurrence of capitalism produces an historically aberrant and unsustainable expansion of the means of production. So if we take tragic possibility seriously, we must admit that the trade-offs will often not be between just and unjust outcomes, but between injustices. That becomes more urgent to face up to as ecological deterioration speeds up and the old patterns of life-building become untenable for most of humanity.

And actually, I have another predicate which is worth clarifying. I don't subscribe to any naive static view of human nature. I think humans have unique capacities, which can result in a wide variety of social types. But I do think that there is a constitutive contradiction, a non-relation as the Lacanians might say, in how societies are made. That there will probably always be costs to civilization, that there will always be antagonism, conflict and dysfunction beyond that which the society can reasonably put up with. There will always be some tragic choices in which sometimes even the freedoms of minorities have to be weighed against the well-being of the whole. And if those tragic choices, as in lockdown situations, make some people angry, bitter and misanthropic, it's possible that they will behave destructively and in a paranoid or malicious or selfish fashion – as some did during the peak of the pandemic. So, the question for me becomes, how do we manage that while living freely?

Perhaps we could take another look at biopolitics. Benjamin Bratton, in his most recent book, engages in a reparative reading of biopolitics. He urges us to reclaim the 'epidemiological model' of society. While it does radically devalue the 'individual' – at least in relation to capitalist mythology of personal responsibility – it doesn't necessarily have to invisibilise poor people, queer people, disabled people, the racially oppressed. It makes us into a network of transmitters and receivers, and we can build infrastructures of care around the information that is generated. We don't have to accept the obscurantism of the market in which social outcomes are unaccountable because their causes are inscrutable, an obscurantism that necessarily generates conspiracist hystericisation (Bill Gates' microchip, the 5G masts, the satanic conspiracy, etc). We can use these surveillance mechanisms to make social injustices visible and accountable, and build aggregated popular will into the responses. We're talking about social intelligence here.

There are a few lines from Prynne's poem, 'Airport Poem: Ethics for Survival', that I like. It's the only one of his poems I've really managed to absorb:

> The heart is a changed
> petromorph, making
> pressure a social
> Intelligence.

The heart is a rock formation, stuck in its ways, resistant to change, yet also changed. And, since a petromorph is already a product of change, to speak of a 'changed petromorph' is either a tautology or a doubling down: changed, and then changed again. By – what? – a 'social intelligence'. A flow, a soft, slow friction: water, gently running, containing just a little grit.

It's coercion, not as brutalisation, not as punishment, not as condemnation or shaming, but as social intelligence. This doesn't solve the problem of, say, protecting minority rights when the community is at stake. In fact, it doesn't solve any problem. What I'm giving you here is a series of questions and intuitions. Because we're only just beginning this work.

About the Contributors

JAMIE ALLINSON teaches politics and international relations at the University of Edinburgh and is a founding editor of *Salvage*. He is the author of *The Age of Counter-Revolution: States and Revolutions in the Middle East* (Cambridge University Press, 2022). He is one of the co-authors of *The Tragedy of the Worker* (Verso/Salvage Editions, 2021).

JAIRUS BANAJI spent most of his academic life at Oxford. He has been a research associate in the Department of Development Studies, SOAS, University of London, for the past several years. He is the author of *Agrarian Change in Late Antiquity* (Oxford University Press, 2001) *Theory as History* (Brill, 2010) – for which he won the Isaac and Tamara Deutscher Memorial Prize – and *A Brief History of Commercial Capitalism* (Haymarket, 2020).

GARGI BHATTACHARYYA lives and works in London and is the author of *Rethinking Racial Capitalism* (Rowman and Littlefield, 2018) and *We, The Heartbroken* (Hajar Press, 2023). A new book on the futures of racial capitalism will be out with Polity this year.

ERIC BLANC is an assistant professor of labor studies at Rutgers University. He is the author of *Red State Revolt: The Teachers' Strike Wave and Working-Class Politics* (Verso, 2019) and *Revolutionary Social Democracy: Working-Class Politics Across the Russian Empire (1882-1917)* (Brill, 2021).

GRACIE MAE BRADLEY is a writer, abolitionist, and novice etcher. She is co-author of *Against Borders: The Case For Abolition* (Verso, 2022).

JACKQUELINE FROST is a writer of experimental prose and poetry and an intellectual historian of French and Caribbean political culture. Her most recent book is *Young Americans* (Pamenar Press, 2022). Originally from Lafayette, Louisiana, Jackqueline lives in Paris.

ALVA GOTBY is a writer and organiser living in London. She is the author of *They Call It Love: The Politics of Emotional Life* (Verso, 2023), and holds a PhD in Media Studies from the University of West London. She writes on feminist theory, social reproduction, housing, emotions, and family, and is active in struggles to abolish prisons and landlords.

NISHA KAPOOR is associate professor of sociology at the University of Warwick. She is author of *Deport Deprive Extradite: 21st Century State Extremism* (Verso, 2018).

JAMES MEADWAY is an economist and host of the weekly *Macrodose* podcast, and co-author of *The Cost of Living Crisis* (Verso, 2023).

RICHARD SEYMOUR is a writer and a founding editor of *Salvage*. He is the author of *The Disenchanted Earth* (Indigo Press, 2022), *The Twittering Machine* (Indigo Press, 2019) and *Corbyn: The Strange Rebirth of Radical Politics* (Verso, 2016), among other books. He is one of the co-authors of *The Tragedy of the Worker* (Verso/Salvage Editions, 2021). His writing can be found in the *Guardian*, the *New York Times*, the *New Statesman* and his own Patreon.

TONY WOOD teaches history at the University of Colorado, Boulder. He is the author of *Chechnya: The Case for Independence* (Verso, 2007) and *Russia without Putin: Money, Power and the Myths of the New Cold War* (Verso, 2018). He is a member of the editorial board of *New Left Review*, and has written on a range of subjects for the *London Review of Books*, *n+1*, the *Nation*, and the *Guardian*, among other outlets.

SALVAGE PERSPECTIVES 13
AUTUMN/WINTER 2022
GIVE DUST A TONGUE

The Return of the Strike

Trade unions, wrote Rosa Luxemburg in *The Mass Strike*, 'cannot permanently maintain themselves in any other way than by struggle'. From that point of view, British unions have been in an existential crisis for three decades.

Until 2022, the level of industrial action in Britain in every year since 1991 – measured by days lost to strike action – was lower than in any year prior. In 2019, the total number of workers involved in a strike hit a record low of 33,000, the lowest number since records began in the 1890s under Queen Victoria. Never before in recorded history has the level of industrial action remained so low for so long.

This grim picture was compounded by the conspicuous failure of all major flashpoints of industrial action following the 1994 signal workers' strike: the wildcat strikes by postal workers in 2002, the two big strikes by firefighters in 2002–3 and 2010, the civil servants strikes in 2007, and the broad but short-lived resistance to public sector austerity in 2011. As the springs of successful action dried up so did recruitment and retention, so that the desert of organisation spread to encompass over three quarters of the workforce: union density falling to 23.1 per cent across the whole economy, and just 12.8 per cent in the private sector, by 2021. And these patterns, far from reflecting the peculiar savagery of

Britain's post-Thatcher settlement, were replicated across the industrial world. They were global, representing the success of an international ruling-class offensive under the rubric of neoliberal globalisation.

In 2022, that pattern was abruptly reversed in Britain, with the biggest strike wave – resulting in the most days lost to industrial action – since 1990. However defensive, however goaded into being by a ruling-class offensive headed by a Conservative Party whose nebulous 'levelling up' agenda has been trashed by the neo-Osbornites now in charge, this represents a vitally important psychological threshold for a long-stagnant British labour movement. The trade unions, out of ingrained demoralisation at least as much as the conservatism of the union bureaucracy, have long behaved as if they were less powerful and more defeated than they actually are. The self-perpetuating reign of internalised defeat now seems to have been decisively punctured.

Nor is this incipient upturn restricted to Britain. According to figures from the European Trade Union Institute, the annual average of days lost to strike action in 2020–21 was more than half what it was in the entire previous decade in France, Spain, Belgium, Finland, Norway and Germany, while in Denmark the figure for 2020–21 exceeded that for the whole previous decade. The major exceptions to this trend are Cyprus and Greece, both of which experienced massive convulsions of near-insurrectionary militancy in the early 2010s, only to be

decisively defeated by financial markets and the European Union. Even in the United States, starting from a much lower base, the number of workers involved in strikes increased by 60 per cent in 2022, according to the ILR Worker Institute's Labor Action Tracker. Workers there began experiencing a modest revival somewhat earlier than their European equivalents, a pattern already visible in 2018 and 2019. However, the general pattern of uptick attests to the unique configuration of global circumstances after the Covid-19 pandemic, particularly the rising costs of energy, supply-chain crises, labour shortages, the legacy of profound state interventions radically reshaping consciousness, and a ruling-class offensive to restrict wages and consumption in the face of inflationary pressures from rising energy and food prices. Altogether, these provided both the incentive for militancy and a unique window of opportunity as worker shortages meant strikes were often settled quickly and in workers' favour, encouraging others to take action.

In this atmosphere of generalised crisis and nascent tumult – punctuated in Britain by the near-suicide of the Conservative Party under the leadership of 'gutsy' (dixit Labour sources) Liz Truss, the calculated indirection of Starmer's leadership of the Labour Party, and punitive interest rate rises by the Bank of England – it was leaders from the most democratically militant quarter of the labour movement, Mick Lynch and Eddie Dempsey of the RMT, who briefly became unofficial media spokespersons for a generalised discontent. Pop-up campaigns, like Don't Pay UK and Enough is Enough, have drawn surges of unexpected support. While Enough is Enough drew crowds of thousands to rallies across the country, building support, over a quarter of a million people signed Don't Pay's pledge to engage in mass non-payment if the government refused to cap energy prices. A poll published in the *Times* suggested that 1.7 million people might refuse payment. The energy firm E.ON warned the government that a non-payment campaign would represent an 'existential threat' to the privately owned energy sector, and it seems likely that such worries contributed to the Truss administration's commitment to cap annual average energy prices at £2,500 per household – catalysing the crisis of the Conservative Party.

The Left initially met this situation in a state of disarray and demoralisation, following the electoral defeat of the Corbyn project and the grave-stamping triumphalism of the Labour right, the Conservative Party, the national media and every other outpost of a wounded and terrified political establishment. However, in the trade-union movement the Left had continued to grow. In 2019, the insurgent candidate Jo Grady won the UCU leadership election on the strength of her campaigning against the attempted sell-out of a strike over pensions by her predecessor Sally Hunt. In 2020, following Corbyn's defeat, the victory of the centre candidate Christine McAnea in the

Unison leadership elections could have signalled the restoration of order. However, the militant candidate Paul Holmes scored a surprisingly strong second place vote with over 33 per cent, a far better showing than any left candidate received in the 2015 election: had the Left united around Holmes, he could possibly have won. In 2021, the shock victory of the workerist candidate Sharon Graham in the Unite leadership election – despite the left vote being split between two candidates and a rabid, tabloid-backed, red-baiting campaign by the right-wing candidate Gerard Coyne – showed that the Right's triumphalism was premature. In the same year, Mick Lynch convincingly won the RMT leadership race with no significant right-wing opposition. Meanwhile, the Royal College of Nurses – an historically conservative union which still has the King as its official patron – has been in turmoil since 2018, when delegates at an emergency meeting voted 'no confidence' in its conservative leadership, starting a dynamic of grassroots pressure for industrial action. This resulted in the union announcing strikes covering nursing staff nationwide for the first time in its history.

As of writing, these strikes are beginning to bear significant, if uneven, fruit. In January 2023, speaking before the Commons transport select committee, the rail minister Huw Merriman admitted that it had cost the government more money to try to break the RMT's strike than it would have cost to settle immediately.

The justification for doing so was to send a signal regarding other public sector pay deals, and to insist on the need for 'industry reform' – referring to the government's modernising maintenance agenda that would shred jobs and conditions. In March 2023, Network Rail reportedly offered a pay rise amounting to a 9.2 per cent increase for the highest paid members and a 14.4 per cent pay rise for the lowest paid, plus 1.1 per cent on basic earnings and backpay, not conditional on accepting the modernising agenda. This does not mean the deal should necessarily be accepted by RMT members. It does not mean that the train operating companies will offer similar pay rises. And the offer is not as generous as it might sound, given an 8.8 per cent rate of inflation over the twelve months to January 2023. But it does mean that, after months of obstructing a settlement, the government's position is weakening. The signs were already there in February 2023, when the Fire Brigades' Union (FBU) was offered a 12 per cent pay rise, an increase from an initial offer of just 2 per cent. Similar settlements are being seen in the private sector, where employees of Drax Hydro Limited won a 16 per cent pay increase. That these deals have been offered in response to the most militant, most disruptive action by, in the case of the RMT, the most demonised sections of the labour movement offers a clear lesson to workers: be demonic.

But there is also a danger of premature triumphalism. Several unions have been willing to call off strike action in the middle of talks, without any agreement on the table. Ambulance workers and nurses suspended their strikes after the government finally agreed to talks. The UCU, whose members have suffered a prolonged decline in real salaries, amounting to 17 per cent between 2009 and 2019, suspended its strike action without any real agreement having been struck. The disarray into which both major factions in the union – both composed largely of politically-minded socialists – have been thrown by the most transparent management manoeuvring demonstrates an old truth: that the politics of union leaders are less important than the militant mobilisation of the rank and file, which in this case has been highly uneven. It would suit the Tories well if the caution of the union bureaucracy and settlements ending the most disruptive strikes isolated the weakest unions and broke the dynamism of the strike wave just as it was proving politically paralysing.

None Shall Pass:
Transphobia Ascendant

As the government seeks to contain its industrial difficulties, it is turning hard toward the 'culture war' frontlines. Conservative deputy chair Lee Anderson admitted in an interview that this was a necessary pivot given that the Tories no longer had Brexit as an issue or Boris Johnson as its bumptious, populist advocate. Among the thematics of officially sanctioned sadism and vengeance are a racist war on migrants instantiated in legislation to 'stop the boats' of refugees crossing the channel, which Home Secretary Suella Braverman calls an 'invasion',

deport those who arrive and ban them from ever returning as refugees. A smaller front is the war on 'woke', or those ineptly derided by Michael Gove as 'radical social change activists'. But perhaps the most novel and toxic tactical foray is in the terrain of transphobic panic.

In January 2023, the British government announced that it would for the first time use Section 25 of the Scotland Act to block a piece of legislation passed overwhelmingly by the Scottish parliament. The Gender Recognition Reform Bill had sought to make it more straightforward and dignified for trans men and women to obtain legal recognition. In line with advice from the World Health Organisation, it permitted sixteen- and seventeen-year-olds to apply for a Gender Recognition Certificate, removed the necessity for all applicants to receive a psychiatric diagnosis of gender dysphoria, and reduced the time period required for an applicant to 'live as' their gender from two years to three months. None of these minimally humane provisions impacted any other piece of legislation. The government claimed that it was incompatible with the Equality Act of 2010, and would negatively impact its implementation: this was simply untrue, as Scottish MSPs had painstakingly crafted and amended the legislation to ensure this didn't happen. Even bracketing principle, the use of this constitutional nuclear option was vastly out of proportion to any possible legal effect of the bill.

What is this about? In part, an exhausted and strategically adrift Tory leadership has been handed an energising campaign issue by a media-generated moral panic. For the last five years, a compulsively vicious British media has alighted on trans women, children and men (in roughly that order) as their latest whipping posts. Newspapers, eschewing trans or specialist insight in favour of incitement, steer their paid attack dogs toward prurient, prudish and puritanical evocations of the dangers to women and children from transgender people. The most flea-bitten, paranoid and sectarian hacks of erstwhile 'radical' feminism, from Julie Bindel to the hitherto obscure Kathleen Stock, are discovered regurgitating the hallucinatory polemics of Janice Raymond and Sheila Jeffreys, are handed column inches to graft onto their careers, and are turned into folk heroes of anti-woke resistance with lavish book deals and television appearances. News anchors, with cynically innocent expressions, pose loaded questions to politicians: Does a woman have a cervix? Does biology matter? Are trans women dangerous in womens' toilets and prisons? Should children be permitted to take gender-affirming hormone treatments?

In 2020, the toothless press regulatory body IPSO released a report on the 'aggressive and damaging' coverage of trans people by newspapers that eschewed trans or expert insight in favour of incitement. One of the most damaging and demoralising aspects of this furore has been the collusion of the liberal press, a chunk of the Labour Party, elements of the trade-union bureaucracy, and even fractals of the Left in the transphobic crusade. In a study for the 2021 UCU conference, on the legacy media's efforts to delegitimise Stonewall for its trans-supportive stance, Dr Gina Gwenffrewi found that the *Guardian* had been a leading belligerent in the offensive.

A segment of the Left is keen to assert the common sense of a reductive materialism, that 'interests' trump 'desires' in the not-very-lonely last instance, and that such culture-war strategy should be understood as deflection, and distraction from 'real' class interests. While there is, of course, a truth to this – deflection and distraction has long been part of the stock in trade of the ruling class against its class enemies – the assertion has always partaken of anxious border-guarding as much as of analysis: the trenchant assertion that such-and-such is epiphenomenal is a code for a plea that we stop talking so much about such-and-such. There should be no question about the importance of locating such oppressive discourses and ideologemes within the context of capitalist profit maximisation. Apart from anything, that is key to unpicking and strategising for liberation within a terrain wherein, far from pitting ruling class against working class, the 'culture wars' divide factions within the ruling-class and capitalism, too, even while they are united with their opponents in the ultimate aim of hegemony. But as with the related and (legitimately or otherwise) stigmatised understandings of the world known as conspiracy theories, this is far from suggesting that such 'culture wars' do not express real material interests, or have very real material political consequences. The Left cannot decorously bypass them to focus on 'real' issues such as wages. Not least because the opposition of 'interests' and 'desires' is utterly unavailing: there is no interest that does not express a prior, intentional orientation toward the world. If 'gender-critical' women claim an interest in not sharing a toilet with a trans woman, it goes without saying that other women, both trans and cis, declare an opposing interest in not living in a transphobic society. Neither interest is entirely without some objective referent, however bent around paranoid phantasmagorias in the case of transphobes, but each is also the expression of a desire. The question is not how 'objective' the interest in discussion is, but how rational. The challenge – and challenge it is – is precisely to integrate such issues as part of a rigorous and anti-moralist approach to these vexed questions, which engages with but does not start and end with them. Or, put otherwise, the task is to discern the precise meaning of these ideological mediations in relation to the totality of the world capitalist system.

Yet the disorienting, disequilibrating effect of the *Sturm und Drang* over trans rights is but one variant in a general contagion of reactionary ideologemes. Chetan Bhatt has astutely suggested that the nascent exsuscitation of fascism in recent years has been conjured up by the metaphysical obsession with 'white extinction'. As 'whiteness' loses its currency as a social and psychological wage, the new far-right literalises this as a 'genocidal' offensive by 'globalists'. Insightful as this analysis is, it does not sufficiently apprise the centrality of sex panic, of which the trans panic is one highly intoxicating (because toxic) facet, to the new far-right and to the authoritarian energies circulating.

This can take a highly traditional, religious form, as in the detectable increase in 'pro-life' agitation outside abortion clinics in Britain. But more often it manifests in a syncretic millenarianism, with proto-religious elements of demonology and redemption as in the QAnon theory that the world is run by a Satanic paedophile conspiracy. And so, at local libraries each week, parents taking their children to the wholesome entertainment of Drag Queen Story Hour have to wade through crowds of reactionary agitators, including QAnon aficionados and members of the would-be paramilitary anti-vaxx group Alpha Men Assemble, maligning the storytellers as 'groomers'. Far-right groups like Britain First regularly lead marches at Dover and provocations targeting hotels housing asylum seekers, partly on the grounds that they contain young men likely to prey on girls. That itself draws on over a decade of insidious news stories, and Labour and Tory MPs from Sarah Champion to Suella Braverman, falsely suggesting that child abuse and 'grooming gangs' are problems particular to Pakistani men. Since the examples cited in these polemics typically include offenders from a range of national backgrounds, it's safe to assume that the word 'Pakistani' is not intended as a geographical reference, but as a euphemism for 'paki'.

Worryingly, this racist sex panic has now produced a number of 'lone wolf' and 'mob' explosions. In November 2022, after a series of far-right marches in the town, a man drove into Dover, firebombed asylum seekers waiting at the port, then drove to a local petrol station and killed himself. His goal, he explained in tweets, was to 'obliterate Muslim children' and 'there [sic] disgusting women'. Then, in February 2023, a crowd of roughly 400 young men gathered at the Suites hotel in Knowsley, Merseyside, and rioted, some using the sledgehammers they had brought to attack police vehicles. The riot was precipitated by viral footage purportedly showing a young man, assumed to be an asylum seeker, chatting up a fifteen-year-old girl. While members of the far-right were present, the organisation appears to have been spontaneous and local. Of course, that revelation was sufficient for Britain's doyens of reactionary inanity, such as Allison Pearson, to set aside usual protocol in describing rioters (typically in the most dehumanising terms possible) and commend them as 'ordinary, decent people' legitimately outraged and unfairly stigmatised as racist by the liberal elite. This was no less than should be expected from a press pack that has been supplying the raw materials for such reactionary shitstorms.

While these iterations of sex panic are local and imbued with specifically British sources of melancholia – such as the inability and unwillingness of the state to protect life during a pandemic or secure consumption during a cost-of-living crisis, or the fact that the poorest citizens of Britain would be better off if they lived in 'poor' Eastern European countries from whence comes the migrant labour so cheaply exploited and demonised, or the fact that Britain is experiencing an epidemic of anxiety and depression driven by precarious living conditions and the palpable experience of facing uncontrollable disasters – they receive their significance, in part, from the global mise-en-scène of sexual anguish. The war on 'gender ideology' initially launched by the Catholic Right has found partisans from Hungary to Brazil. The Proud Boys hail the Taliban for recovering their country from 'globohomo'. Hindu nationalists accuse Muslim men of seducing Hindu girls with a 'Love Jihad'. The Christchurch murderer reiterates the mantra of Muslim 'birth rates', their fecundity apparently suggesting a worrying potency in contrast to a whiteness enfeebled by global liberalism. One of the main incitements to recreational, manifesto-touting massacres is the perception that the loneliness of the young male is due to the world's domination by sexually proficient Chads and Staceys who refuse to share the sex fairly. The pervasive and multicausal experiences of vulnerability, violability, disorientation, dissatisfaction and demoralisation are being consistently and symptomatically figured as problems in the sexual order.

That the impulse to restore existential order – sent askew by the pathologies of capital accumulation reaching new limits without finding solutions sustainable even for the relatively short-term, the intensification of inter-imperial rivalries under the pressure of ecologically-induced energy and supply crises, the decomposition of political hegemony as representative institutions self-consciously evacuate themselves of representative content the better to exclude the untrustworthy popular classes, the loneliness and distrust engendered by the growing precarity of life-building and the evisceration of common spaces, and the epistemological crisis brought on by the ever more effective subsumption of knowledge production by private capital – manifests itself as a drive to violently reinstate cisheteronormativity, is surely significant. That Britain – with its singularly stagnant political culture, intellectual philistinism, and position of relative decline in both the international division of labour and the imperialist chain – should be so taken even on parts of the Left with images of trans subversion, is no less so.

New Cold War: Weather Balloons and Tanks

In early February 2023, the US government and national media embarked on a paranoid bender about the intrusion into the US of veritable flotillas of minatory Chinese balloons. It began when, on 4 February, the US Navy shot down a Chinese balloon hovering in US airspace off the coast of South Carolina, on the orders of Joe Biden. In the ensuing weeks, there followed a flood of media speculation that the balloon was part of a Chinese spying programme, demands from NBC and the *New York Times* to repel the aggression, and claims of a 'balloon gap' in which the inscrutable foe had a lethal edge over Washington. Several more flying objects were shot down on Biden's orders. Nor, it was disclosed, was this the first assault wave of Chinese balloons. There had been others before, scandalously disregarded under both Biden and his equally sinophobic predecessor. It has not been established conclusively that the balloon was a spycraft, and Biden quietly admitted that all the other objects shot down were probably operated by domestic companies or research bodies rather than the Chinese.

This collective hallucination and pant-wetting recalled nothing so much as the late and unlamented 'Havana Syndrome', in which a bipartisan political and media consensus asserted that a range of minor idiopathic symptoms experienced by several US government and military personnel were the result of a global enemy campaign. So subtle was this campaign that it could not be localised, for the symptoms erupted everywhere, from New Delhi to Washington, DC. Anonymous intelligence officials briefed journalists that Russia was likely to blame, but they could not be sure. Eventually, the story reached an absurd yet characteristic apotheosis when the CIA quietly confirmed that the symptoms were not the result of a campaign by a rival state. It may be that, just as the famous 'Puerto Rican syndrome' expressed a thwarted rebellion on the part of Puerto Rican soldiers drafted to the US military, these various ailments somatically literalised a troubling apprehension of imperial vulnerability among the personnel. Either way, as in the balloons farago, otiose statesmen along with serried ranks of manicured national security reporters and their shadowy 'sources' had conjured out of miniscule data a national syndrome that made the porosity of American power abruptly vivid.

Such are the pathologies of decline, which is felt everywhere. During the Trump administration, several international journalists of both neoconservative and liberal-imperialist complexion had exhibited a lachrymose sense of post-Washington melancholia: the US, they complained as Trump trashed the doctrine of 'multilateralism', no longer wished to lead, or even to hold their hands through the world's unfathomable darkness. And notwithstanding their relief at Biden's election, his subsequent withdrawal from Afghanistan, more or less on Trump's schedule, elicited an outcry of similar bourgeois discontent.

But when, a little over a year ago, Moscow undertook the patently irrational gambit of invading Ukraine, and then made a series of unforced military errors in doing so, it seemed like the old gang was finally getting back together. Biden, despite his initial reticence, soon declared that he was prepared to spend billions on a long war in Ukraine. Boris Johnson was briefly in his element as the sort of Churchill-impersonator you might have ordered from Wish. Macron, increasingly beleaguered domestically, took his 'Jupiterian' strut to the world stage. NATO was delighted, almost immediately presented with new applications for membership from historically neutral Sweden and Finland. The poetasters of eternal Cold War, such as Anne Applebaum and Robert Kagan (who enjoys some connections to the Biden White House) were thrilled by the opportunity for that shrill bellicosity which is ever misunderstood as 'moral clarity'. Ukraine's president, Volodymyr Zelensky, was the ideal ally for this confederacy: an autocratic liberal and a former celebrity with an excellent sense of public relations, whose position as the international representative of a nation attacked and oppressed by Russian imperialism made him instantly relatable on all social industry networks. Narcissistic empathy for 'people like us' enabled a felt solidarity that required no thought whatsoever. Out came the Ukraine flags, decorating all feeds, and featured on pubs and homes in middle-class English suburbs.

And yet, over a year on from Vladimir Putin's deranged and murderous gamble – the aims of which are still scarcely intelligible if one assumes the slightest strategic intelligence in the Kremlin – the afflatus has gone out of the thing. There is little to show for either the US or Russia, as there is simply no sign of either Moscow or Kyiv achieving its stated objectives. Notwithstanding the augmentation of Usonian and European military budgets and the international commitments of weapons, rockets, tanks and eventually aircrafts to Ukraine, and notwithstanding the obvious disarray of Russia's armed forces, Putin does not appear to be running out of steam or new lines of attack. It is hardly plausible that Ukraine could outright defeat the Russian military, but is also unbelievable that Russia would achieve anything but a pyrrhic victory. The International Criminal Court has issued a warrant for Putin's arrest over his war crimes, but it scarcely carries any credibility: neither Russia nor the US are signatories to the Court, it has never prosecuted or even inconvenienced a war criminal of any serious clout, and its activity largely consists of tackling politically easy cases of alleged war criminals from sub-Saharan Africa.

Finally, and this is where the balloon frenzy reveals itself as a form of displacement typical of dreamwork, the US may not even get much say in a negotiated settlement if the stalemate persuades Putin of the need for a face-saving deal and Zelensky of the need to moderate his official Russophobia, which has been manifest in extraordinary laws banning the main opposition parties for being pro-Russian. In late February 2023, to the dismay of Washington and NATO's headquarters in Brazil, but eliciting the cautious endorsement of Kyiv, the Chinese government published a twelve-point position paper on the resolution of the conflict in Ukraine. Calling for 'all parties' to respect 'the sovereignty of nations' under international law, rejecting sanctions on Russia, and criticising 'expanding military blocs' (obviously NATO), it suggested that China would mediate between Kyiv and Moscow in securing a ceasefire and negotiated settlement. Volodymyr Zelensky was circumspectly positive about Beijing's 'respect for our territorial integrity, security issues', and his deputy foreign minister welcomed the proposal. Three weeks later, in mid-March, talks hosted in Beijing resulted in a new deal between Saudi Arabia and Iran. China's role as mediator had been kept secret until that point. The shift in relations between Saudi and Iran is already leading to palpable geopolitical results, with a Saudi delegation present in the Yemeni capital Sana'a to discuss with Iran's Houthi allies the possible end to the savage war in Yemen. The extent to which China's role is causal is obviously unclear, but – at the very least – it is centrally involved in this new moment.

The disclosure of its involvement, and Ukraine's reaction to its initiative, suggested two worrisome things for the United States. First, Zelensky's hitherto belligerent response to calls for negotiations, which in one interview included entertainingly dismissing Putin as a 'nobody', may have concealed a deeper anxiety about the prospects, and the limits of Western support. Biden and NATO allies may be willing to munify a 'long war', but they are not willing to risk direct engagement with Russia in order to tilt the balance decisively in Ukraine's favour. The fact that Ukraine is open to such overtures suggests that they'd quite like a way out. Second, Zhongnanhai could do far more damage by exploiting Washington's hegemonic decline than through the fetchingly nineteenth-century technique of dispatching a hot air balloon to get an executive view on the enemy. For, just as Washington could not possibly be received as a good-faith arbiter of dialogue between Saudi Arabia and Iran – given its long-standing friendship with the Wahhabi theocracy and sabre-rattling at the Islamic Republic – it is also difficult to see how Washington could be accepted as a sensible third-party in a war that it has been funding and arming. If there

is to be a ceasefire, and if there are to be negotiations, then Chinese state-capitalism – which remains, trade wars aside, massively intricated with US capitalism – looks like a more plausible winner than either Moscow or Kyiv.

This, it must be acknowledged, is a highly perilous situation. The decomposition of traditional Washington's neoliberal world order, coupled with ascendant nationalism and the periodic crises produced or inflamed by climate disaster from pandemic to energy crunch, have all intensified and been intensified by imperialist rivalries in recent years. The Biden administration, while no doubt eager to exploit Moscow's substantial self-inflicted damage to its assiduously cultivated international reputation for brutal efficacy, has done almost everything it has with an eye to its rivalry with China, from expansive industrial investments to stimulate domestic capital accumulation and adapt the system to the new era of ecological crisis, to escalating tariffs on Chinese goods going far beyond anything Trump imposed, to desperate efforts to undercut Chinese commercial and diplomatic influence in the African continent. The US military is currently engaging in the largest joint military exercises with the Philippines in years, under Ferdinand 'Bong Bong' Marcus Jr, while the Chinese government has engaged in its own military drills, simulating strikes on Taiwan – which it considers to be its territorial possession.

The intensification of inter-imperialist rivalries pivots far more on the strange co-dependence and conflict between the US and China than over Russia. For example, while the US and China are engaged in a face-off over Taiwan, Macron has visited China with the European Commission president Ursula von der Leyen, who articulates the executive, class-wide perspectives of the European bourgeoisie. While wrapping up lucrative trade deals, Macron reiterated the doctrine of 'strategic autonomy' – first articulated by European Union rulers in relation to Trump – and insisted that Europe must not become a 'vassal' for US interests. He also lent his verbal support to a potential Chinese role in mediating between Russia and Ukraine. This complicates any 'new Cold War' narrative, since the clarifying global bipolarity that directed and constrained imperialist antagonisms in the period from 1945 to 1990 are no longer there. The relative decline of the US, and the self-conscious 'autonomy' of Europe, make the dream of refounding Cold War alliances an exercise in imperial nostalgia. That is what is so dangerous: the further the US falls, the more Europe vacillates and the more 'global China' eludes US efforts at encirclement, the more likely are further expostulations of nationalist hysteria and further advances from farce to tragedy.

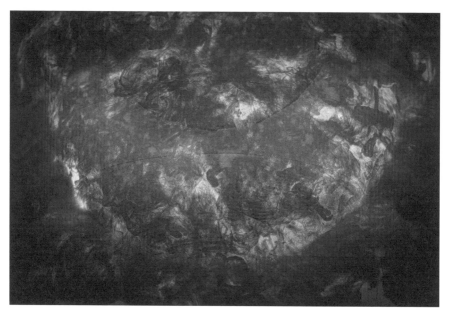

Energy Famines and 'Natural' Disasters

In Kahramanmaraş, in Şanlıurfa, and in Aleppo, the February 2023 earthquake along the East Anatolian fault struck buildings knowingly not designed to withstand such tremors, and they fell fast, in pancake-fashion. A total of 41,156 people were killed in Turkey and a further 5,801 in Syria.

The East Anatolian fault is a 'strike-slip' fault. The Arabian plate pushes north against the Anatolian plate, which pushes westward. The horizontal friction as – propelled in their motion by heat generation from the decay of radioactive elements deep inside the planet – they grind together, builds up as seismic energy. If it is not regularly discharged in earthquakes, the debt will be paid in more and bigger earthquakes in the future. This is an unavoidable, catastrophic aspect of the earth's energetic system, and the majority of the Turkish land mass is permanently at high risk of earthquakes.

There is, notoriously, and even when the most catastrophic natural forces are loose, no such thing as a 'natural disaster'. As earth scientist Ben Wisner and his colleagues have been documenting for years, every earthquake, flood, famine, wildfire and storm is conditioned by a cluster of vulnerabilities that are 'man-made'. Of the 1976 Guatemala earthquake, which killed 23,000 people and injured 76,000, Wisner et al write in *At Risk*:

> The physical shaking of the ground was a natural event ... However, slum dwellers in Guatemala City and many Mayan Indians living in impoverished towns and hamlets suffered the highest mortality. The homes of the middle class were better protected and more safely sited, and recovery was easier for them.

And so it is in Turkey and Syria, where earthquakes have been far more lethal than other major quakes in Northridge, California or Kobe, Japan. Despite lower maximum intensity of ground-shaking, and lower population density, recent earthquakes on the East Anatolian fault have killed more because the power of the inertial forces created by the energy conducted into the structures of the buildings easily overwhelmed the poor reinforcements and displaced the different floors of the buildings. The result was that, when the buildings collapsed, the floors were tightly packed together, leaving so little space that the chances of finding a breathing body in the wreckage was in most cases negligible.

While earthquakes are unavoidable, decades of Turkish state policy of cramming the working class and millions of Syrian refugees into cheaply built, poorly designed and often illegal apartments constructed by corner-cutting developers in the most dangerous earthquake zones could have been avoided. Equally avoidable was the refusal to impose elementary earthquake-proofing in the design, and the retrospective legalisation of illegal constructions by Erdogan's 2018 'zoning amnesty law'. And what certainly could have been avoided was the triumvirate of counterinsurgent bombing campaigns waged from Damascus, Moscow and Washington, DC, which so devastated Aleppo that the surviving residents were forced to construct new and unsteady homes out of the salvaged ruins.

'Natural disasters' may, but do not necessarily, beget 'disaster communities' of the sort about which Rebecca Solnit has written. As the sociologist Kai Erikson describes in his study of collective trauma, there may be a wave of euphoric fellow-feeling among survivors, but in the aftermath communal faultlines can be prised wider apart, forming a social chasm of blame and bloodletting. So it has been in Turkey where, within days of the disaster, social industry campaigns driven by Turkish fascist Ümit Özdağ started to scapegoat Syrians for looting, stealing aid or even causing the disaster, spawning outbursts of mob violence and harassment – sometimes resisted, we note, by countervailing outbursts of solidarity. Scarcely days after the disaster, moreover, the European Union introduced 'tougher' rules for 'irregular migrants', extinguishing hope for many of those refugees. 'Natural disaster', then, enfolds within it not just the social massacres concomitant on class, imperialism and racism, but the casual bureaucratic cruelty of Enlightened liberalism and the kind of theodical nationalist reasoning – evil comes from the outsiders – that perpetuates further miserable death and ruin. This is a chronotope of the climate future, as the constitutively catastrophic propensities of the earth's energy system are catalysed by capitalogenic carbon emissions, and hypertrophied by capitalism's systemic cheapening of poor, black and migratory life.

Since the beginning of 2022, the chronic crisis in the earth's energy system has erupted in the predictably acute form of floods in Pakistan, eastern Australia and California, raging wildfires in California, Arizona, France, Morocco and Texas, deadly heatwaves in India, Japan and Pakistan, droughts in China, and typhoons in the Philippines. In each case, the source of the surplus of wild, destructive energy driving such 'extreme weather' comes from the addition of what Joseph Fourier called 'dark heat' – infrared radiation reflected from the earth's surface having absorbed solar radiation, and trapped by carbon molecules in the atmosphere – to the earth's system.

Wildfires, for example, are a natural occurrence on a planet packed with organic fuels in the soil, carbon-based organisms and an oxygen-rich atmosphere. Annual peaks of solar radiation routinely, as a matter of ecological balance, burn up the grasslands and forests of Australia, California and Siberia. Even in Britain, heathland and moorland need small, regular wildfires to thrive. But on a hotter planet, the wildfires are becoming more frequent, more intense, and are themselves releasing more heat energy into the atmosphere. The average heat energy released by annual western wildfires in the United States, for example, is 1.4×10^{18} Joules. But in 2020, wildfire season released 5.6×10^{18} Joules of heat energy, enough to supply the world's energy demand for four days. Half-way into 2022, the wildfires in Europe were already 273 per cent above the average for a whole year. Wild energy, disproportionately loaded into the earth's system by the 100 corporations responsible for 71 per cent of annual emissions – and even allowing that those corporations have outputs, employees and consumers, the effective power to emit is in their hands – sets up predictable yet stochastically distributed 'natural disasters', calamities which are then compounded by structurally distributed vulnerabilities.

It is a proof of the intrinsic anarchic wastefulness and misallocations of the fossil capitalist system that, even as surpluses of wild energy are pumped into the earth system, human populations experience energy shortages and global price inflation without equivalent in recent experience. The proximate causes of shortage are in no case 'natural'. They include a short-term decline in oil and coal investment as a result of recent commodity price crashes, the preeminently ecological crisis of the Covid-19 outbreak which resulted in sharp economic contraction and rapid rebound stressing energy supplies while also delaying maintenance work (in, for example, North Sea oil extraction), and Russia's imperialist war on Ukraine and inter-imperialist rivalry with Washington resulting in energy sanctions and restricted gas supply from Gazprom to Europe. The banal dynamics of capitalist investment driven by expected profit rates, prices determined mainly by supply and demand, and access determined by state policy, created this energy crisis.

We even hear talk of 'energy famine', a concept that first popularised during the OPEC crisis of 1973-74. In September 2022, in the deepest trough of the energy crisis, John Gray warned of a potential 'energy famine' coming to Europe. In the United States, the ecomodernist, nuclear-shilling Breakthrough Institute warns of 'electricity famine' as local providers facing energy shortfalls resort to rolling blackouts. But, like the devastating El Niño-triggered food famines discussed in Mike Davis' *Late Victorian Holocausts*, energy famines do not arise merely from scarcities. They result from the way scarcities are produced and mediated by markets, property rights and states. That is why there was no 'energy famine' in Europe, where most states – often under pressure from mobilised citizens, as in Britain's Don't Pay campaign – resorted to expedients such as price controls and subsidies to

insulate their electorates from the worst. Given the chaos of the earth system, energy famines are likely to become a more pervasive reality in the future, but to understand them aright one must first talk about the work/energy regime, and systems of unequal energy exchange (capitalism and imperialism).

The work/energy regime is essential. The energy that is available to us is a result of labour processes, from mining and refineries to supply chains and distribution. As Andreas Malm reminds us in *Fossil Capital*, 'No piece of coal or drop of oil has yet turned itself into fuel ... fossil fuels necessitate waged or forced labour – the power of some to direct the labour of others – as conditions of their very existence.' More fundamentally, the purpose of energy in a capitalist system is to enable more work: minimum energy in, maximum work out.

The same austere logic of capitalist efficiency was a primary source of the El Niño food famines that, as Davis documents, made the 'Third World'. As drought struck British-ruled India, for example, colonial administrators insisted on withholding aid as far as possible, on the grounds that it would be an inefficient deployment of caloric resources. Where aid was distributed, it was tied to demands for back-breaking labour. Refugees fleeing the stricken countryside were expected to travel to camps, from whence they would be deployed as 'coolie labour' on railroad and canal projects. Davis is even able to tell us what was considered an adequate minimum of calories for their rations: 1627 calories a day was considered sufficient for heavy labour in Madras, about half of the minimum that Bengal labourers needed fifteen years previously. Minimum energy in, maximum work out.

Relations of unequal energy exchange also magnified the crisis to Biblical proportions. The railroads that the British poetasters of the 'free market' had supposed would ensure an efficient distribution of food had actually been used to speed stocks out of India to England during the years of plenty, because English farms had suffered reduced yields. Internal relations of unequal energy exchange also prevailed, as the same rail networks were used to ensure that what stocks remained were shuttled from drought-stricken regions to whichever populations could pay the highest price.

Similar dynamics will determine who suffers from energy famines in the future. The hoarding of stocks of gas and coal, and the privileged access that imperialist states have to those resources, is only the beginning of the problem. Electricity, which may be produced by renewable energy sources as much as by burning coal, is not the sort of physical object that can be hoarded as stock. It is a mediated, social and cultural thing, distributed through normative structures of access embedded in pylons, generators and undersea power cables. The pre-eminently capitalist solution to energy famine in the 'Third World', much as it was to the integration of the 'First World' working-class into

the system, has been 'access' to the grid. Yet access to the grid, in India, South Africa and Puerto Rico, has not meant effective access. In these cases, effective access depended on non-commodified pricing, public ownership or regulation – practices which have generally been foreclosed by the regime of neoliberal globalisation. In Puerto Rico, for example, the energy famine resulting from Hurricane Maria in September 2017 was conditioned by exorbitant pricing as empire-produced dependence on imported fossil fuels resulted in the highest energy prices in the US. As a result, the state energy firm, controlled by the same oil giants that sold oil at elevated prices to the country, had accumulated unpayable debts totalling $9 billion. On the eve of the storm, it had declared bankruptcy, and the privatising vultures were circling. As a result, months after the hurricane 40 per cent of Puerto Rican households were still without electricity.

This is not to say that a 'true' energy famine is impossible in a rich, imperialist democracy. For example, Texas suffered an energy famine over two years ago amid severe winter storms, not because of energy shortages in the United States but because of a privatised, streamlined-for-profit energy system and the corporate-aligned politics of Texan administrators who deliberately made the state an 'energy island' so that it wouldn't be subject to Federal regulations. Where energy famine occurs, it will be caused not by shortage, still less by the absence of nuclear power, but by a confluence of property relations, state policy and market imperatives potentiating the catastrophic latencies in the earth's energy system and then choking off supplies, above all to the working class. The energy crisis is, as ever, a crisis born of what Jason W Moore calls capitalist world-ecology.

Cancelling the Apocalypse?
The Global Economy

In the twilight of 2022, the lands resounded to wailings and the gnashings of economists' teeth. The outlook for the world was widely understood to be particularly grim. In October 2022, the IMF limned 'the weakest growth profile since 2001 except for the global financial crisis and the acute phase of the Covid-19 pandemic'. The aftermaths of those epochal shocks, dramatically exacerbated by the devastating energy crisis and supply-chain impact following Russia's war with Ukraine, would see inflation at a generational high, and a severe cost-of-living crisis. Overall, the world economy was 'experiencing a broad-based and sharper-than-expected slowdown', with growth forecast to slow from 6 per cent in 2021 to 2.7 per cent in 2023. Though not technically a recession, this would, the IMF warned, 'feel like one'. This was particularly the case given the immense unevenness in the world economy: the IMF saw US growth likely to slow to 1 per cent, Britain to 0.5 per cent and Germany entering recession.

And the IMF predictions were among the most optimistic of

mainstream commentators'. The WTO predicted growth of 2.3 per cent, the OECD and UNCTAD (the United Nations Conference on Trade and Development) 2.2 per cent. No wonder that two thirds of the economists polled by the World Economic Forum in January 2023 saw a global recession as likely, and one fifth as extremely likely.

Of course, with the predictability of sunrise, the policies that such mavens advocated for in response were overwhelmingly acts of class war.

Thus, for example, the remorseless focus on tightening interest rates, usually with reference to what the economist John O'Trakoun, of the Federal Reserve Bank of Richmond, has dolefully called the 'doom loop'. This is the notorious 'wage-price spiral', whereby rising workers' wages lead businesses to raise prices, thus fuelling inflation overall. This nostrum of holy bourgeois writ has seen new life in the post-Covid-19 recovery, which gave workers a degree of leeway to demand better wages. In mid-2022, *Forbes* magazine added propheteering to profiteering, to warn that 'We Need To Talk About The Worker Wage-Price Spiral Before It's Too Late', as if its readership were not already voluble on that very topic. In June 2022, Boris Johnson warned that '[w]hen a wage-price spiral begins, there is only one cure and that is to slam the brakes on rising prices with higher interest rates'. The UK's Chief Secretary to the Treasury, Simon Clarke, warned that 'if we end up in a world where … all settlements try to match inflation or

even exceed it then we are … actually creating the conditions whereby those expectations become baked in. … That is the inflationary risk.' A more decorously expressed version of the concern – and one, to be fair, that stood alongside other less imaginary economic bugbears – lay behind the governer of the Bank of England, Andrew Bailey, calling for workers' 'restraint' when it comes to pay rises, and the Bank's continued rise in interest rates. That is, to put it plainly for the sake of 'the economy', workers have to get poorer in real terms.

Such ruling-class strategies prioritise the weakening of the working class – the ruling class' class enemy, that is – over any amelioration of the global capitalist economy, even on its own terms. That the narrow focus on raising interest rates risks recession, for example, is hardly news. Nor is it news that this is often the explicit aim: Paul Volcker, a pin-up of the hardest version of this strategy, proclaimed in 1979 that '[t]he standard of living of the average American has to decline'. So, *mutatis mutandis*, today: November 2022, the governer of New Zealand's central bank, Tim Scott, agreed with a Finance and Expenditure select committee that the bank was deliberately engineering a recession, though he did dream fondly of a 'job-rich slowdown'. The world's largest asset manager, BlackRock, warned in its 2023 Global Outlook that central bankers 'are deliberately causing recessions by overtightening policy to try to rein in inflation', making 'recession foretold'.

Such anti-inflationary norms are predicated, to varyingly overt degrees, on that wage-price spiral. What's telling is that even according to capitalism's own more honest analysts, that spiral is imaginary. As the IMF itself put it in November 2022, in a comprehensive analysis of wage and price movements over the last six decades, '[w]age-price spirals, at least defined as a sustained acceleration of prices and wages, are hard to find in the historical record.'

The point is not that inflation should be of no concern to the working class. What is not imaginary, of course, is the weakening of labour represented by its decreasing share of value. And this is the point of these policy prescriptions, rather than any that might relatively benefit the working class over capitalists, such as price controls, rent control, caps to CEO pay, or higher taxes on the rich and corporations. 'What if', as Hadas Thier puts it, 'instead of raising prices, businesses just made do with smaller profit margins? After all, US corporations are currently making record profits, posting their fattest margins since 1950.' As Société Générale strategist Albert Edwards has recently argued, a 'primary driver of this inflation cycle is soaring profit margins', making it what he calls 'greedflation'. As resistant to mere facts as ever, though, capitalist central banks are mostly staying the interest-rate course.

Such questions, however, might initially seem less pressing than they were some months ago, after the immediate threat of recession abruptly receded.

A combination of a warm winter and better-than-feared oil and gas reserves have minimised the projected energy shortages; consumer spending has remained higher than expected; and the Chinese economy has opened after its Covid-19 lockdowns. The EU Commission now predicts that Europe will evade 'technical recession' in 2023, and the IMF has raised its forecast for global growth to 2.9 per cent. And in the US, the unemployment rate recently fell to its lowest rate in over half a century.

These phenomena are real and important, and the outlook for the global economy has improved. But it remains weak, uncertain and highly uneven. The devil is, as ever, in the details.

The flurry of relief is at figures that, globally, are way below pre-pandemic figures (roughly 3.8 per cent growth per year during the 2010s), which were, in turn, below the average before the recession of 2008. Geographically, half of the forecast expansion is expected to come from China and India alone. The major advanced economies are forecast to see growth slowing to 1 to 2 per cent, and the Eurozone only 0.7 per cent (a tiny rise that obscures great variety within). The economy of the Britain itself, a particularly failing state, is set to be particularly badly placed over the forthcoming months. The Bank of England only reversed its forecast of recession in March 2023, and then only declared the likely narrow avoidance of a 'technical recession'. As the website economicsobservatory.com damply put it, these figures 'mean that the country's economic performance in 2023 might not be quite as weak as previously expected.'

China itself is aiming at growth of 'around 5 per cent', roughly in line with World Bank predictions. Considerably higher than most of the rest of the world this may be, but this is the state's lowest target in decades. This reflects what the ratings agency Moody's has described as the 'headwinds' it faces, including the deeply unstable international environment, increasingly ill-tempered competition with the US, a shrinking working population and the results of a vast property bubble. Even if, as many analysts committed to the Kremlinological decoding of signals from Beijing assert, this 5 per cent figure is likely an acceptable floor rather than a rigorous prediction, this is a clear attempt to manage expectations, and a reset of standards for the regime of accumulation. The era of Chinese capitalist mega-growth is effectively over.

If that implies, however, that China may not replace the US as the most powerful economy on the globe soon, or ever, as many prognosticators have been predicting for some time, that is not any evidence of the strength or stability of the US itself. Even in these less-bad-than-expected days, its economy is in a parlous state. As Michael Roberts has shown, the US' reduction in unemployment and uptake of jobs is more an artefact of statistics than evidence of a healthy economy. 'January [2023]', he writes, 'saw a statistical adjustment that added in an extra 1.6 million to add to the payrolls that had been missing from data'. And the shift in Americans in full-time work between March 2022 and January 2023 was zero: the figure for both months was 132.6 million. Part-time jobs, however, rose by 1.5 million: what is deemed the labour market's 'strength' is a situation in which workers are forced into part-time work – much of it casual – and wherein, as the cost-of-living crisis continues, many will have to take two or three such jobs to survive.

Already, it is beginning to look as if reports of the death of the US recession have been greatly exaggerated. Jobs added in February 2023 were lower than Wall Street expected. Layoffs are up fivefold in a year – and are a giddying 38,487 per cent higher in tech than they were a year ago, bespeaking the end of yet another bubble. The high-profile collapse of Silicon Valley Bank, the largest bank failure since 2008, is not a high-profile anomaly but, as even the business press acknowledges, a possible warning of more trouble. 'How deep is the rot', the *Economist* asked in March 2023, 'in America's banking industry?'

Which takes us back to those interest-rate rises, to which the Fed remains committed – if not with the fervour some ideologues demand. They will, of course, do less than nothing to address these problems. Indeed, as one CNBC commentator puts it, echoing Marxist common sense and the declarations of monetarists themselves, 'as the central aim of the Fed's inflation fight, a recession may well be a feature, rather than a bug, of current monetary policy'. This is only 'irrational' if one understands the role of economic stability, bracketing even equality or the delivery of necessary goods and services, as the most important job of central banks. As soon as one is clear that that is a nice-to-have at best, but that the disciplining of the working class is non-negotiable, these policies seem less deranged.

None of this, of course, is to say that a recession will definitely occur 2023, or even next. It is, though, to insist that the rush of 'good economic news' this year is tissue-thin, and the situation unstable and dangerous. Marxists are sometimes upbraided by our opponents for our jeremiads, for seeing crisis everywhere we look, for never allowing that things might improve. Improve they might, and to deny that is not socialist theory. There is a key difference between the countless capitalist ideologues – who predict, regular as metronomes, that the boom-bust cycle is over, that happy times are here again, that the doomsayers are definitely wrong – and the socialist critics – who insist that any such reversal will itself reverse, that the situation is inherently crisis-ridden and will inevitably get worse again, at great human cost. The former claims have been proved false, and the latter correct, literally 100 per cent of the time, throughout human history.

Tragically, however, for all that rectitude, a faith that underlies some socialist prognostications on these points is, in fact, quite wrong. A certain Marxist catastrophilia can be predicated on the comforting belief that once the situation gets bad enough, the only way is up. Late capitalism is a constant, brutal proof that that does not follow. There can be badness and catastrophe all the way down; apocalypse without redemption.

'THIS WAGER ON THE
IMPROBABLE NECESSITY
OF REVOLUTIONISING THE
WORLD IS VERY LIKELY ONE OF
MELANCHOLY.'
—DANIEL BENSAÏD